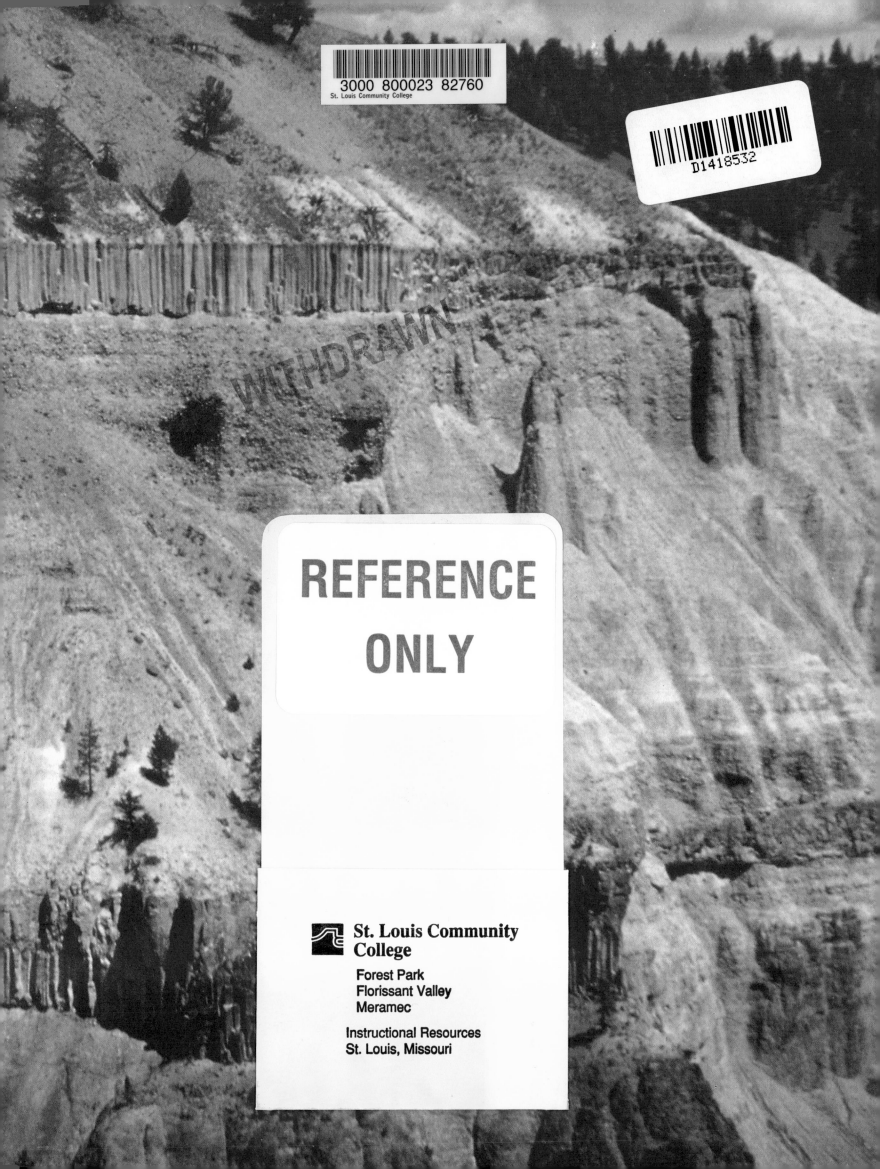

AN ILLUSTRATED GUIDE TO

ROCKS & MINERALS

AN ILLUSTRATED GUIDE TO

ROCKS & MINERALS

MICHAEL O'DONOGHUE

This edition first published in the United States in 1992 by
SMITHMARK Publishers Inc., 16 East 32nd Street,
New York, NY 10016

Published in England by Dragon's World Ltd,
Limpsfield and London

SMITHMARK books are available for bulk purchase for sales
promotions and premium use. For details write or call the manager
of special sales, SMITHMARK Publishers Inc., 16 East 32nd Street,
New York, NY 10016. (212) 532-6600.

ISBN 0-8317-6389-2

EDITOR Michael Downey
DESIGNER Ann Doolan
ART DIRECTOR Dave Allen
EDITORIAL DIRECTOR Pippa Rubinstein

Typeset by Dragon's World Ltd
Printed in Spain

CONTENTS

PREFACE

While rocks make up the surface of the earth, minerals make up the rocks. A rock may be composed of a number of different minerals or contain only one mineral species. Compared to the number of plants or animals there are not very many different kinds of rock nor mineral, and it is not difficult to learn about those important species which are either familiar from daily observation or which form prominent exhibits in museums. This book is intended to introduce some of the major rock and mineral species in the hope that their beauty will make the reader want to know more about them, and the way in which they indicate how the planet was formed. As soon as you can, go into the field – after, or even before, reading this book.

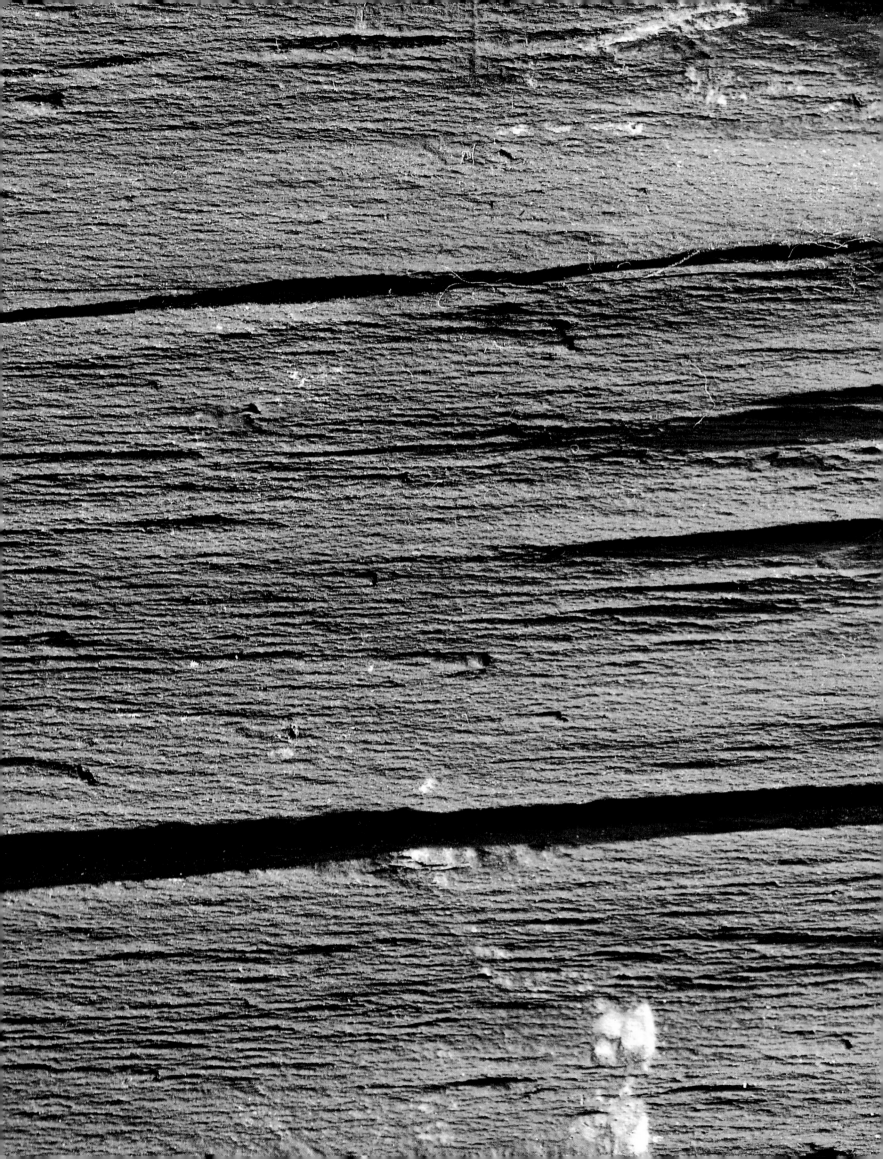

PART ONE

ROCKS

The study of rocks, petrology, is concerned with the material to which many fine crystal specimens may be attached. All rock (the mineralogist calls matrix what others call rock) is composed of minerals, the commoner rocks containing fairly small numbers of different species. If you are looking for minerals you have to know the right kind of rock to look for as minerals are usually associated with particular types of rock; it would not be very profitable for the collector to search basalts for beryl, or granite for halite. Three rock classes are universally recognized – igneous, metamorphic and sedimentary.

The cliffs of Bonaventure Island, off the Gaspé Peninsula in Canada, display bedding planes characteristic of sedimentary rock.

IGNEOUS ROCKS

M olten rock material is called magma. It is formed in the mantle of the earth and moves upwards to the surface. When solidified magma is injected into rocks near the surface it forms igneous intrusions. When magma reaches the surface still in its molten state (as when a volcano erupts) it forms lava which spreads out over the surface. Some igneous intrusions form batholiths, dykes and sills. Batholiths are large in every way: they may extend for hundreds of square kilometres and their final depth is hard to establish. Stocks are smaller intrusions; plugs are fairly small cylindrical intrusions which frequently occur in the channels by which volcanic material passes to the surface.

Dykes are vertical or near-vertical sheet-like intrusions which cut across the country rocks (those rocks established before a geological event like an intrusion); sills are horizontal and are parallel to layers in the rocks that they cut. Major intrusions cool down fairly slowly on account of their large size and great depth. For this reason their constituent minerals tend to form large crystals. This assemblage gives a coarse-grained rock known as plutonic rock. Quicker-cooling minor intrusions have a finer texture.

Diorite

Extrusive rocks, on the other hand, are formed from material poured *over* the surface (intrusive rocks are igneous intrusions into existing country rock). Lavas may spread far from their source or remain localized, building up the characteristic volcanic shape. Gas in the magma may come out of solution if pressure is reduced when the melt approaches the surface. The gas may form bubbles in the lava which become vesicles in the rock. Pyroclastic rocks are made from fragments of lava blown apart by gas pressure; very large pyroclastic fragments are known as *bombs*; the grain size is very small in volcanic ash. Volcanoes are made from lava flows and pyroclastic rocks.

The rapid cooling of extrusive rocks means that the minerals in them have only a limited time to crystallize (some do not, like obsidian, a natural glass). Minerals are fine-grained but larger crystals occur when the magma starts to crystallize before it is erupted, giving large crystals in a finer-grained matrix. Here the large crystals are called *phenocrysts* and the whole rock has a porphyritic texture. Sills and dykes are often made up of porphyric rocks.

Igneous rocks are classified on the basis of their main constituent minerals of which seven predominate. These are quartz and the silicate groups feldspar, feldspathoids (minerals with composition and structure close to the feldspars but not actually members of the feldspar group), pyroxenes, amphiboles, micas and olivine. Other

Basalt

up of a single mineral, as olivine in dunite rock and pyroxenes in pyroxenite. It is rare for some minerals to occur together in igneous rock – quartz and olivine are not usually found together. We shall see elsewhere that the main igneous rock minerals are in fact mineral groups of closely related species. The table below summarizes the main rock-forming minerals in igneous rocks:

Leucocratic minerals
quartz
feldspars   members of the feldspar group
feldspathoids   leucite, sodalite, nepheline, cancrinite

Mafic minerals
olivine
pyroxenes   members of the pyroxene group
amphiboles   members of the amphibole group
micas   members of the mica group

Hornblende gabbro

The mineralogist will always check in a specimen to see if quartz or feldspar are present and how much there is of pyroxene, amphibole, olivine and biotite – these are the dark or *mafic* minerals. Light minerals such as quartz, the feldspars and the feldspathoids are called leucocratic and their proportions are also measured in a specimen. Igneous rocks are also classified in accordance with their grain size; coarse-grained rocks come from the plutonic rocks of large intrusions and medium- to fine-grained rocks from minor intrusions and extrusive rocks. Granite, syenite, diorite, gabbro, peridotite form a series in which there is a change from low mafic to complete mafic content. Granite and syenite are light in colour, diorite and gabbro dark, and peridotite black or dark green.

In some plutonic rocks we may find areas in which the minerals form much larger crystals. These areas are frequently lens-shaped or occur as veins. These areas of coarser mineralization are called *pegmatitic segregations* and can occur in granite, gabbro, nepheline syenite and other rocks. The minerals, though forming larger crystals, are the same as those in the surrounding rock. These areas are not the same as pegmatites. When a magma has a low viscosity the early-formed crystals, usually denser than the magma, sink to the bottom of the magma chamber where

they accumulate. As the composition of the magma changes so different minerals will form and their crystals will settle on the lowest layer. This layering can often produce valuable ore minerals, such as chromium.

Sometimes a plutonic rock will have a finer-grained texture than normal and the phenocrysts it contains in those circumstances will often be well-shaped crystals. This is because they started growing early on and were not confined by other crystals during their growth. Examples are

Granite

Andesite porphyry

habit) allows the formation of well-shaped (euhedral) crystals. Some crystals attain very large sizes – quartz crystals over five metres long are recorded. The thickness of pegmatites may vary from a few centimetres to many metres and they can often be found at the outer margins of granite stocks or in the country rocks.

Elements found in the residual fluids of granite and nepheline syenite magmas are silicon, aluminium, sodium and potassium (in the main) which are concentrated at the pegmatite stage because they form ingredients that melt at the lowest temperatures. Additionally there is a group of less common elements which began by being dispersed in the magma but which later on concentrated in the residual fluids. They tend to form minerals late in the process as their ions are the wrong size for incorporation into the principal rock-forming minerals. These elements include boron, phosphorus, fluorine, chlorine, sulphur, lithium, beryllium, rubidium, caesium, molybdenum and the rare earth elements.

Pegmatites usually contain quartz, alkali feldspar, plagioclase feldspar and muscovite. In nepheline syenite pegmatites the quartz is often replaced by one of the feldspathoids, usually nepheline. Many granite pegmatites are characterized by 'graphic granite', an intergrowth of quartz and orthoclase resembling writing. Granite pegmatites also show such minerals as beryl,

sanidine in trachyte, orthoclase in granite, orthoclase and quartz in rhyolite, olivine, augite and plagioclase in basalt and plagioclase in andesite.

Pegmatites

When the crystallization of magma in a major intrusion is coming to an end the residual melt becomes concentrated, containing water, chlorine, boron and other elements that have not already been used up by the minerals that have already crystallized. The melt gradually turns to a watery solution as crystallization goes on and this solution is more able to penetrate cracks in the already solidified rock mass; sometimes the melt penetrates the country rocks as well. These solutions crystallize as the bodies known as *pegmatites* and the crystals they contain are large since the melt is relatively fluid. Pegmatites contain a number of rare minerals and are sometimes characterized by drusy cavities. In these cavities crystals grow inwards from the

Rhyolite

chrysoberyl, apatite, brazilianite, tourmaline, spodumene, topaz, danburite, microlite and petalite. In nepheline syenite pegmatites we find aegirine, eudialyte, natrolite, analcime, chabazite and the black form of andradite.

Hydrothermal Deposits

When the magmatic solution from which a pegmatite is formed has given up most of its constituents to pegmatite formation there will still be a residual fraction. This will be a water-rich fluid rather than a magma. These hydrous fluid phases are often found in magmas with granite to diorite compositions in the final stages of crystallization. Forcing their way into the country rocks the fluids deposit their constituent elements. Rocks in which this has happened are rich in a number of minerals, in particular metallic ore minerals. The deposits are called hydrothermal.

Some hydrothermal minerals are economically important and include many metallic sulphides such as pyrite, galena, chalcopyrite, sphalerite, marcasite, tetrahedrite, bornite, arsenopyrite and stibnite. Traditionally other hydrothermal minerals were collectively known as *gangue*, a term which once designated minerals of little or no economic importance. Today these minerals are of greater importance since uses for them have multiplied. They include fluorite, quartz, calcite, barite, siderite, dolomite and rhodochrosite.

In studying hydrothermal mineral deposits some idea of the temperature of formation can be gained. Low-temperature hydrothermal deposits (epithermal) are formed in a temperature range of 50–200°C, mesothermal (medium-temperature) 200–300°C, and hypothermal (high-temperature) at 300–500°C. The different groups merge into one another but in general the hypothermal deposits are closer to the source of magma with the other two types further away. Hypothermal deposits provide gold, magnetite, ilmenite, cassiterite, scheelite, garnet, mica, apatite, tourmaline and topaz. Mesothermal deposits may contain gold, galena, chalcopyrite, pyrite, sphalerite, bornite and tetrahedrite. Epithermal deposits may contain pyrite, marcasite, cinnabar, stibnite, silver, pyrargyrite and proustite.

Hydrothermal deposits often take the form of veins as the solutions take paths through the rocks, usually through fissures. One of the

Obsidian

commonest fissures is the fault plane; additionally joints and bedding planes, with volcanic pipes, provide channels for hydrothermal solutions. Though veins are very characteristic of hydrothermal deposits, most such deposits come about by metasomatic replacement. This involves the dissolution of the original rock minerals and their replacement by new ones. This can take place over very wide areas.

Rocks at and below the surface are weathered

Nepheline syenite

carbonates which contain oxygen. At greater depths the primary hydrothermal deposit will be reached in vein or massive deposit form.

We can see that there are two parts to the oxidation zone. Near the top minerals are dissolved and removed. Oxidized ore deposits are formed as the cold leaching solutions travel down and their contents precipitate. In this way much of the metal content of the solution is now concentrated at the bottom of the zone rather than being distributed through the whole of the oxidation zone. Some metallic deposits are formed thus.

Dissolved metals which do not precipitate in the zone of oxidation travel down to below the water table and are there deposited as secondary sulphide minerals. This area is thus enriched so that what were originally rather poor sulphide deposits may become worth working. Erosion of the surface lowers it with the water table and the zone of oxidation, so that the secondary sulphide deposit will once more be oxidized and its metals carried down.

At volcanic fumaroles minerals can be seen growing. These are formed from gases which were originally dissolved in the magma but which have been released into the surrounding rocks, thence to find their way to the surface. Substances from the gases are deposited round the fumaroles. A common mineral formed in this way is sulphur.

Mineral aggregates deposited in gas cativities in lavas are called *amygdales*. In the amygdales the crystals grow from the walls inwards so that well-formed examples are fairly common. Zeolites in particular are found in amygdales as well as quartz, calcite and chalcedony.

Geodes, a variety of amygdale, are usually filled with silica minerals, especially with banded agate or contain a centre core of amethyst. In *enhydros* water can be heard moving about inside. This is presumably the remainder of the fluid from which the quartz or chalcedony formed. Minerals deposited by hot springs are also classed as hydrothermal and include calcite, siliceous sinter, ochreous forms of iron oxide and opaline silica. The water from which the minerals are deposited is very dilute as it will already have lost many of the elements it once contained. Many metallic and non-metallic elements are carried in solution by these hot springs and they are usually deposited as sulphides, as in a Californian mercury deposit.

Peridotite

and the sulphides of hydrothermal deposits are particularly affected because they are unstable at near-surface conditions. Water, carbon dioxide and oxygen act together to cause mineral decomposition and oxidation. Oxidation of sulphide minerals gives sulphuric acid and sulphates which also cause further decomposition.

Rock components are taken into solution and carried down to lower levels, hydrothermal deposits losing their sulphides to leave a rock rich only in silica and iron oxides. These rocks are known as *gossan*. Weathering stops at the water table and there is a deficiency of oxygen below that. This means that minerals carried down are deposited as sulphides, rather than sulphates or

Syenite

METAMORPHIC ROCKS

Heat, pressure and the addition or subtraction of elements are features of metamorphism, the process by which existing rocks are altered by later geological events. In general metamorphic minerals grow in solid surroundings so that crystals tend to crowd one another. This means that quartz, feldspar, calcite and dolomite do not usually attain the well-formed crystals that are characteristic of their occurrence in other types of rock. Other minerals, however, produce perfectly formed crystals at the expense of their neighbours and these crystals are called *porphyroblasts*. Garnet, staurolite, kyanite, epidote and andalusite are characteristic porphyroblastic-forming minerals.

Two types of metamorphism are regional and contact. When linear belts of the earth's surface become geologically active, with the deposition of very thick sediments and the gradual formation of mountain chains, it is apparent after erosion of the raised material that rocks underlying it have been metamorphosed before the process of elevation. The rocks are said to have been *regionally metamorphosed* and they may extend over thousands of square kilometres. *Contact metamorphism* takes place over a much smaller area and is confined to the immediate area of igneous intrusions. Magma at temperatures in the range of 700–1200°C forms intrusions in the existing rocks, heating and altering them. The process creates a metamorphic aureole which may range in size from several kilometres down to a few centimetres. When there

Gneiss

Marble

petrologist can work out the pressures and temperatures at which metamorphism took place. Rocks associated with the pressures imposed during mountain building are seen to be folded as in schists and gneisses – the crystallization of the constituent minerals under stress accounts for the foliation. Contact metamorphic rocks are formed at high temperatures but low pressures and give a *hornfelsic* texture which is even and granular, since the minerals in the rock do not take up a preferred orientation.

The names given to metamorphic rocks indicate their structure and mineralogical content:

Slate has a single prominent cleavage and is fine-grained and homogeneous. The cleavage is not related to the bedding.

Phyllite also has a fine grain, coarser than the grain of slate. The prominent cleavage surfaces show a greenish or silvery sheen.

Schist has a coarse grain with marked foliation and contains plenty of elongate minerals like the micas.

is mineral subtraction from, and addition to, the rocks close to the intrusion the process is known as *contact metasomatism*. Rocks known as *skarns* are produced in this way.

Regional metamorphic rocks are graded according to how much they have been metamorphosed. The grade may be low, medium or high. As the metamorphic process proceeds new textures are formed in the rocks – but it may still be possible to recognize features of the original igneous or sedimentary rock, such as fossils in the latter. By examining the new textures the

Phyllite

Gneiss has a coarse grain with a structure of darker and lighter layers. Quartz and feldspars are the usual minerals.

Hornfels has a fine grain and even texture with no cleavage and no schist-like lamination or foliation. It results from contact metamorphism and may contain porphyroblasts.

Quartzite is a rock composed mainly of recrystallized quartz.

Amphibolite is mostly hornblende with a variable plagioclase content.

Marble is composed of recrystallized calcite or dolomite with a coarse to medium grain.

Schist

Skarn is rich in calcium, magnesium and iron minerals and is formed by the contact metasomatism of limestone and dolomite by plutons of granite of intermediate composition.

Contact Metamorphic Rocks

The minerals crystallizing in contact aureoles are determined by the composition of the original rock and the degree of metamorphism that has taken place. This means that different minerals will be found in the outer part of the aureole from those found in the immediate area of the intrusion where the temperature is higher. Many different assemblages can occur, however, and the fineness of some of the grains makes the determination of the constituent minerals a task for the microscope.

Contact Metasomatic Rocks

Here the igneous intrusion helps in the formation of volatile elements which pass into the country rocks to form new minerals. The volatiles are mostly water, boron, fluorine and chlorine. Boron forms distinctive rocks when it is introduced by metasomatism into shales and slates – the rocks are tourmaline-rich. When the country rock is an impure limestone (that is, a limestone containing some shale and sandstone) it reacts with boron-rich volatiles to give datolite and axinite, which is frequently associated with andradite and hedenbergite. This may also happen in the case of some igneous country rocks. When fluorine is in the metasomatizing fluids it produces lepidolite,

Quartzite

phlogopite and muscovite micas, chondrodite, clinohumite and fluorapatite in impure limestones. Where chlorine is present scapolite group minerals are formed. Metasomatic rocks associated with nepheline syenites are characterized by alkali-rich minerals such as alkali feldspars, and alkali-rich amphiboles as well as aegirine and aegirine-augite.

Skarns produce a number of interesting minerals because volatile elements migrate upwards during their formation along with sulphur, silicon, potassium, sodium, magnesium and metallic elements. The metals are usually oxides or sulphides making skarn deposits a good source

Skarn

for the mining of their ores.

When sedimentary rocks are intruded their structure influences the skarn body. Metasomatizing fluids enter through bedding planes, especially those dipping towards the intrusion, and faults also provide a ready means of ingress. Masses of rocks such as limestone which extend downwards into the intrusion from the roof may become detached and form *xenoliths* floating in the magma. Skarn deposit minerals include andradite and grossular of the garnet group, wollastonite and pyroxene. Metallic minerals may include magnetite, hematite, pyrite, chalcopyrite, bornite and pyrrhotite.

Regional Metamorphic Rocks

This is a very complicated group of rocks since so many different kinds of existing rock can be metamorphosed and so many different minerals arise at different temperatures and pressures. Four factors account for the minerals found in regional metamorphism: the composition of the original rock; the pressures and temperatures involved during the metamorphic process; the type of metamorphism; and circulating fluids. Shale is one of the common rock types to be metamorphosed. As metamorphism increases, shale changes to slate, phyllites and then schists.

At successively higher grades minerals appear of metamorphism. One such mineral succession is chlorite, biotite, almandine, staurolite, kyanite and sillimanite.

If we look at rocks other than shales we find different mineralogies. Basic igneous rocks that have been metamorphosed will give chlorite, albite, epidote, sphene, calcite, hornblende, biotite and almandine. An impure non-dolomitic limestone (that is, one containing no magnesium) may show, on metamorphism, zoisite, grossular, vesuvianite, diopside and scapolite. Metamorphosed dolomitic limestone may give forsterite of the olivine group, minerals of the serpentine group, spinel, diopside, hornblende, tremolite-actinolite, phlogopite, chondrodite. Metamorphosed peridotites are rich in serpentine minerals, talc and tremolite, but not in olivine. These are only a few examples of many possible ones.

Serpentine

SEDIMENTARY ROCKS

S edimentary rocks are formed at the surface and are not subject to high temperatures and pressures like the other two rock classes. Some are made up of the remains of weathered older rocks and are gradually hardened by accretion in processes of lithification and diagenesis.

An important weathering process involves ground water in complex reactions and different minerals are affected. Quartz is hardly altered by weathering while feldspars are more affected. The mafic minerals, the amphiboles, pyroxenes and the micas are easily decayed. The process involves the formation of new minerals, many being rich in water, and many clay minerals are formed. Sodium, potassium, calcium and magnesium may go into solution, and these elements in solution, the new and the unaltered minerals, are the material from which sedimentary rocks are

Fossiliferous limestone

Faulted limestone

Flint

formed. Such material is often transported by wind, water and ice to accumulate in the sea.

Rocks of mechanical origin include the fine-grained clay minerals – hydrous aluminium silicates which are not usually collected. Minerals of alluvial deposits or *placers* are concentrated when their host rocks are weathered away. These include corundum, topaz, rutile, gold, diamond and the platinum minerals.

Rocks of chemical origin include minerals not found in other kinds of rock. The minerals are either formed directly by primary precipitation or are formed by chemical reactions in the sediment, the reactions being induced by percolating solutions. In the first group are calcium and magnesium limestones, pure silica rocks, iron rich sediments, rocks rich in phosphorus and the evaporites which mostly comprise chlorides, sulphates, carbonates and nitrates.

Many limestone rocks are formed by precipitation from sea water direct, or with the addition of matter derived from living organisms. Calcite and aragonite are the chief minerals. The precipitation of iron from solution gives rise to rocks known as ironstones. Hematite and magnetite are the most prominent minerals with other iron compounds. Silica deposition gives the rock called chert, made up of chalcedony, opal and finely crystallized quartz. Flint differs from chert in being found in nodular masses and not as bedded deposits. Phosphorus deposition gives phosphate rocks with a suite of phosphate minerals, apatite being the most prominent.

Evaporites precipitate from concentrated brine in enclosed bodies of salt water such as saline lakes or from seas cut off from the main oceans. Most minerals are chlorides, sulphates and

Calcareous tufa

Shale

Chert

concretions. The desert roses made of gypsum and barite form in this way. Limestones may be formed from the calcareous skeletons of living organisms and, in some cases, constituent fossils may be replaced by pyrite or other minerals. Fossilized wood may sometimes occur as jet and some vivianite is formed from bone deposits of recent times.

carbonates of calcium, sodium, potassium and magnesium. Gypsum, anhydrite and halite are the most common minerals. Non-marine evaporites provide nitrates, boron and iodine compounds.

Nodules of a number of minerals arise from chemical reactions in the sediment after deposition; pyrite nodules are some of the most commonly encountered. Cementing of rock by silica or iron oxide concentration gives rise to

Conglomerate

PART TWO

MINERALS

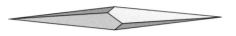

Minerals are the substance of which rocks are made. They vary in size and appearance; many occur as powders and encrustations while others are found as spectacular crystal groups or large single crystals. There are almost as many types of mineral collector as there are types of mineral and the following section describes some of the techniques of collecting, emphasizing that care needs to be taken with the preservation of important sites and of one's own safety. Collectors should be members of a recognized and efficient group – this is the best way to learn.

Copper is mined from this large open-pit mine at Bisbee, Arizona, USA. Bisbee is one of the world's best locations for copper minerals.

Scientists have often found it difficult to define objects in words and mineralogists have had to be content with a description of a mineral as a naturally occurring inorganic solid substance with a definite chemical composition which varies only within precise limits. This means that each mineral species has its own chemical composition which can vary a little but which with a larger variation would become a different species. Over the years mineralogists have found that many species are related and can be ascribed to groups or families; the relationships are chemical and structural and there are many instances in which one species grades into another.

There are just over 3,000 individual species known and new ones are being identified at the rate of at least one a week. The rate of increase in identifications is due to the increasing sophistication of instrumentation; the electron microprobe has replaced wet and dry chemical analysis and the use of the blowpipe. This does not mean, though, that the older methods of identification have become irrelevant – the large and expensive instruments are quite rightly not used for routine identification and even today there are limits to what they can do. Many minerals can be safely identified in the field using very simple tests like streak and hardness.

Minerals have a variety of uses and many museums have collections of economic minerals. These include metallic ores and minerals with ornamental uses such as gemstones. Many other species are too small to see with the eye alone and their value may be more academic in that they serve to point out the temperatures and pressures obtaining at the time of their formation. Such information is very useful when more important minerals are being sought. Here the relationship between minerals and rocks needs to be considered.

Rocks are made up of minerals, sometimes of a single mineral but more usually of a number. The best known rock is probably granite in which the individual crystals of quartz, feldspar and mica can be seen with no difficulty. Other rocks are so fine-grained that their composition is harder to work out. Thin sections are cut and examined

Cerussite (Utah, USA)

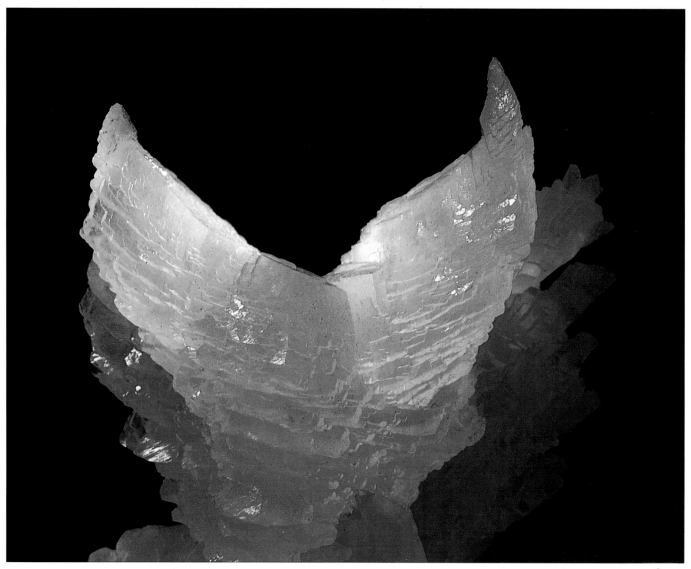

Calcite (Chihuahua, Mexico)

under the microscope in a variety of lighting conditions which show up the crystals of the minerals composing the rock. Generally speaking, the science of rocks – petrology – is harder to conduct in the field when detailed examination of specimens is needed. Mineral specimens give away their identity more easily and many can be identified on sight.

Collecting

It is not always easy to find minerals in the field and later on we shall see some of the difficulties and how they may be overcome. It is easier to see them for the first time in museum collections where the finest specimens will be on view; in this way you will be able to know what you are looking for when you get into the field. While some collections concentrate on the economic uses of minerals, others simply show them as natural substances. Such collections used to be called cabinets of minerals from the time when they were formed by individual connoisseurs. Some of these have now developed into collections of international importance, such as those of the Natural History Museum in London, and the Smithsonian Institution in Washington. Anyone wishing to begin the study of minerals must become familiar with at least one of the major cabinets; even the arrangements of such collections are instructive since there is more than one scheme by which specimens can be displayed. Most major collections are arranged in chemical order and this can be followed with the aid of a textbook arranged in the same way.

Visits to places where minerals can be found are often hard to arrange because safety aspects have to be paramount. In any case, it is quite hard to find the minerals you are looking for once you are at the right place – the working face of a mine is a confused, noisy and dusty scene and tiny specimens only come to light after washing or chemical treatment. Only accredited visitors will be allowed underground or at the working faces of open quarries, so it is better to visit the dumps; however, care needs to be taken even here.

The collector should make a point of looking at quarry faces or cliff sections. These will be especially important in areas where there has been past tectonic disturbance. Quartz and calcite crystals can be found in joints and faults and minor mineralization may occur along discontinuities in the sequence of rocks. Blasting may reveal new material. For example, in recent years rare lead oxychloride minerals have been found in manganese veins in the Mendips of south-west England – the veins follow former fault directions. Collectors should look out for road construction works in igneous or metamorphic terrains; sometimes gypsum crystals can be found in clays.

There are many ways in which you can begin to study minerals but a combination of visits to the field with experienced collectors, visits to museum collections and membership of a well-run mineral club will bring the greatest satisfaction. Many minerals are easy to recognize and this gives the student an early confidence so that when he eventually tries to identify something which looks like grey dust, he will have some idea, from the circumstances in which it was found, what it might be. The following chapters examine some aspects of minerals in detail, so many of the more important ones will become familiar.

This volume is not intended as a textbook but it is hoped that the pictures and the descriptions will encourage readers to turn to specialized texts, the more important of which are listed in the bibliography. The study of minerals can be carried out in isolation up to a point but it is strongly recommended that the serious reader try to get in touch with people of similar interests as soon as possible. This is best done by joining a club, of which there are quite a number. Although the standard can vary greatly, the best are very good indeed. When looking for a club (addresses are usually obtainable from the local library or from specialist museums) try to find one with a varied and ambitious programme, which includes a good number of outside speakers. Such a club will run specimen evenings and field trips on which you can learn a great deal.

Collecting in Mining Areas

For reasons of safety and lack of time for visitor supervision, it is very rare for the amateur to be allowed into a working mine. The collector will usually do best by prospecting the mine dumps or keeping an eye open for civil engineering projects such as road cuts as these may open up valuable deposits.

Mines from which metallic ores are extracted will probably give the best specimens. Examples are bournonite ('cog-wheel ore') from Cornwall and pyrite from Panasqueira, Portugal. Fluorite from the lead mines of the northern Pennine ore-field and calcite from Cumbria, both in England, are still sought by collectors, although they were gangue minerals (that is, not those sought for processing and sale). At one time specimens were preserved by miners, but modern mechanical methods of ore treatment do not allow for much of this. When the desired ores have been extracted, the remaining slurry is disposed of. Not all mines, however, are cavalier about fine crystals and a growing number in many countries have seen the potential for specimen sales.

In some former metalliferous mining areas collectors may find secondary minerals associated with the main ore and gangue minerals. Fine examples of such minerals have been found in Cornwall, England; specimens include bournonite from the Herodsfoot mine, chalcocite from mines in the Redruth area and cuprite from the Phoenix mine. Calcite from Wheal Wrey, St Ives, forms long, twinned prisms. The collector may find new localities for specimens in small pegmatites and granitic intrusions once checked for their economic value but found to be of little worth. Such sites include lithium mines in San Diego county, California, now famous for fine tourmaline crystals, and the Varutrask pegmatite in Sweden and the Hagendorf pegmatite in Germany which give interesting phosphate minerals. The Meldon aplite in Devon, England, used to produce such minerals as axinite and tourmaline. Aplite is a fine-grained, granite-like rock.

MINERAL CHEMISTRY

Minerals take their particular appearance and their physical and optical properties from their chemical composition. This chapter looks at atoms and at the way in which they combine to give a range of structures which in turn give the final shape to mineral crystals. We look at the way in which atoms become electrically charged and how this process allows atoms to pack together. We also look at solid solutions, characteristic of so many important mineral species.

Petrified wood from the Petrified Forest, Arizona, USA. The structure of the original wood remains after its replacement by silica.

A study of mineral chemistry must begin with the atom, the smallest particle of an element to retain all that element's properties. Elements themselves are the simplest substances that chemical techniques can isolate. There are more than 100 known elements, though many are not involved in mineral formation. The element gold can combine with other elements but it cannot be split up into more fundamental metals. An atom of gold can be split up into smaller particles but these fragments would not be gold. Atoms are measured in nanometres ($1nm = 10m^{-9}$).

The particles into which an atom can be split are protons, neutrons and electrons. Protons and neutrons have approximately similar masses and occupy the nucleus at the centre of the atom. Neutrons have no charge, while protons are positively charged. Orbiting the nucleus are negatively-charged electrons and their charge equals the proton's positive charge. Overall atoms are not charged as they contain equal numbers of protons and electrons. The mass of an atom resides almost entirely in its nucleus, but most of its volume is occupied by its cloud of electrons.

Although the traditional conception of the electron cloud as planets orbiting the sun does not entirely accord with present-day knowledge, it does provide a convenient picture of the movements of electrons. This movement can be predicted as the electrons traverse known paths. In the nucleus the number of protons is balanced by the number of the orbiting electrons. The number of protons varies from one in hydrogen to over 100 in the heaviest elements. This number is known as the atomic number. In all atoms, except hydrogen, the protons in the nucleus are accompanied by neutrons – the number of neutrons need not be the same in all atoms of an element. Strontium atoms have thirty-eight protons but from forty-six to fifty neutrons. The variable examples are known as isotopes of strontium.

The atomic weight of other elements is defined as the weight of one of its atoms compared to that of an atom of hydrogen. This weight is very close to the weight of the single proton in its nucleus since the weight of a single electron is approximately $\frac{1}{1836}$ of the weight of a proton or neutron. When we look at a table of the atomic weights of all elements we see that they are not all whole numbers. This is because any element may have several isotopes and the atomic weight is the average weight, taking the isotopes into account. The standard atomic weight taken is based on one carbon isotope, ^{12}C, which is 12.

Electrons orbit in up to seven discrete tracks called shells which are lettered alphabetically from K to Q outwards from the nucleus. Each shell has a limit to the number of electrons it can contain (two for K, thirty-two for N) and the lighter elements with up to eighteen protons in their nuclei fill their shells systematically outwards. Hydrogen, with one nuclear proton, has a single orbiting electron in the K shell. Lithium, with three protons, has a full K shell with a single electron in L. The elements up to argon on the periodic table of the elements fill their shells following this pattern; argon has eighteen protons. After argon the elements with higher atomic numbers break the pattern, letting some electrons into outer shells before the inner ones are filled.

The inert gases, so called because they are almost impossible to combine chemically with other elements, have eight electrons in their outermost shell; other elements are regarded as chemically stable if they can attain a similar outer shell content. In short, the inert gas configuration seems to be an ideal for elements to aim at. In order to attain this ideal state, atoms use their electrons commercially by trading them with other atoms so that their electron clouds can become identical to those of the inert gases.

This trading of electrons is very important as substances derive their chemical nature from it. The trading is in two stages: atoms of the element gain or lose electrons until they attain the configuration of the nearest inert gas. This process leads to atoms becoming electrically charged and they are then known as ions. Those ions which have gained electrons in their search for inert gas identification are negatively charged anions; those which have lost electrons are cations with a positive charge.

The number of electrons gained or lost by an element in this process is known as its valency. For example, sodium (Na) and fluorine (F) have one more and one less electron respectively than the nearest inert gas on the periodic table, neon (Ne). Their ions are written Na^+ and F^-. They are monovalent, Na^+ being a cation and F^- an anion. Magnesium (Mg) has two more electrons than

Liddicoatite (Anjanabonoina, Madagascar)

Rhodonite (New Jersey, USA)

neon. By losing both it becomes a divalent cation written Mg^{2+}. These examples with electronic configurations fairly close to those of inert gases form only one kind of ion. Others (such as carbon, C, and silicon, Si) have atomic structures midway between two inert gases. Carbon can either gain four electrons to become C^{4-} to resemble neon or lose four electrons and become C^{4+} resembling helium. Carbon in nature can be either an anion or a cation. Where elements have incomplete inner electron shells, they can form ions with several valencies. Iron (Fe) can form as Fe^{2+} or Fe^{3+} depending on circumstances.

The electrical charge of the proton keeps adjacent atoms apart by mutual repulsion. When two atoms link, the actual joining is carried out by the interaction of their outermost electrons. This joining or bonding can take place in three different ways. Ionic bonding involves two elements forming ions of equal and opposite valency. The spare electron or electrons from one atom separate from it and fill the vacancies in the outer shell of the other atom. The pair of ions formed are held together electrically. Groups of ions can also be linked in this way; for example, a divalent cation with two univalent anions.

The covalent bond shares electrons; two or more atoms coming close together share electrons in such a way that both effectively have eight in their outer shells. Metals have a metallic bond in which the ions pack closely together and leave their outermost, loosely bound electrons free to move about independently. This enables metal to be beaten into thin sheets or drawn into wires. It also accounts for their electrical conductivity. Covalent and ionic bonds are strong, the former established in specific directions around an atom and the latter non-directional. It is also common for bonds to be intermediate between the two. Solids containing ionic or covalent bonds are relatively rigid.

When the linked atoms are of different elements, a chemical compound is the result. In many minerals sub-groups of atoms are bonded strongly together in a predominantly covalent way, forming complex ions (radicals). A common example is the tetrahedral arrangement of four oxygen atoms round a single atom of silicon to give the complex anion written $(SiO_4)^{4-}$. These clusters of atoms bond together ionically with single atoms or other groups in a variety of minerals.

The complex anion $(SiO_4)^{4-}$ must be bonded to a cation or cations with a total valency of 4 to get an electrically balanced compound. Two atoms of the divalent metal Mg would fit and the mineral forsterite has the composition $Mg_2(SiO_4)^{4-}$. This is written here in shorthand but it could be written $(Mg_2)^{4+}(SiO_4)^{4-}$.

How are atoms built into minerals? Looking at water we see that it can occur as a solid (ice), liquid (water), or gas (steam). Temperature dictates which forms at a particular time. Heating a material causes the atoms to vibrate faster, thus breaking the bonds between them. In this way the independent H_2O groups in steam (the groups are called molecules) move freely. They are loosely linked in water and rigidly bonded in ice, forming a crystalline structure. Although ice shows little structure to the eye, a snowflake has obvious hexagonal symmetry.

In glass a molten mixture of minerals is cooled so quickly from the molten state that loose interatomic bonding of the liquid melt is established before it has time to organize itself into a crystalline structure. In nature few substances have this 'frozen' atomic structure. One example is the glassy rock substance produced when

Lazurite (Georgia, USA)

volcanic material is quenched. Glassy material is also produced when the feldspar mineral plagioclase is struck by meteorites. When this happens, the bonds of the plagioclase are shaken and disrupted. Such a mineral is common on the Moon but rare on Earth, where meteorite strikes are less common. Substances which do not have the atomic order of crystals are known as amorphous and they do not show the properties associated with direction which are characteristic of crystals. Opal and natural glass are amorphous.

Crystals are made up of ions which can be described as having the shape of spheres. These cannot easily fit together without leaving space in between (as bricks in a wall). This problem is solved in two stages. Firstly, ions of differing sizes are combined into small groups which can be imagined as simple solid shapes with flat faces; they are known as coordination polyhedra. These polyhedra can pack together, thus forming the crystal.

There are several kinds of polyhedron: imagine a pea surrounded by oranges. The best fit is three oranges around one pea. Draw this, join up the centre points of the oranges and you get a triangle. The common complex ion $(CO_3)^{2-}$, the carbonate ion, has this shape. If a larger sphere replaces the pea, four oranges can fit around it and the shape is therefore a tetrahedron – the shape of the silicate anion $(SiO_4)^{4-}$.

As the ion within the polyhedron increases still more, the ions around it increase to six and the polyhedron becomes the octahedron shape – two pyramids joined base-to-base. When the small ion reaches the size of the ions surrounding it, the shape becomes a cube. When ions are of equal size, they can link to form a crystal without forming polyhedra first. They are arranged in differing patterns which are known as close packing. Coordination polyhedra and close packing apply most commonly to crystals with ionic or metallic bonding, as there are non-directional bonds between the crystals. The oriented bonds in covalently bonded crystals usually follow the same direction as the principal axes of the polyhedra so that these basic atomic groupings can be recognized in covalently bonded minerals.

When a material gets hotter under geological conditions, its atoms, vibrating faster, are more able to fit into loosely packed crystal structures. Pressure compresses the electron clouds and denser crystals are formed as a result. The compound SiO_2 can crystallize in five different major structures which are known as polymorphs of SiO_2. Diamond and graphite are polymorphs of carbon; in graphite the carbon atoms are linked to form sheets which slide over each other; in diamond, which is the high pressure polymorph, the carbon atoms are held together by a three-dimensional network of rigid, tetrahedrally-oriented covalent bonds. This structure gives diamond its hardness, toughness and density.

The size of ions determines the crystal structure adopted by a mineral. Many pairs of ions are similar in size and can take each other's place in a mineral, leaving its structure unchanged. Minerals with an identical crystal structure are said to be isomorphous. In some special cases we find a solid solution. In the olivine group of minerals the pure magnesium and the pure iron members are forsterite (Mg_2SiO_4) and fayalite (Fe_2SiO_4). If a mixture of these two is melted and allowed to cool, the crystals which form are neither one nor the other but rather a single olivine containing both Mg and Fe. It is as if the forsterite and the fayalite had dissolved in each other, hence the name 'solid solution'.

There is a complete series (known as an isomorphous series) between the two end-members, forsterite and fayalite. Similar series can be found in many other mineral groups. In the case of olivine the magnesium–iron series is written $(Mg,Fe)_2SiO_4$. When the olivine contains seventy-five per cent of the forsterite component, this can be shown as $(Mg_{0.75}Fe_{0.25})_2SiO_4$.

Solid solution is critically affected by temperature because atoms vibrating faster at high temperatures have the effect of stretching the crystal structure and loosening the bonds. Then the structure can accommodate ions that would be too large to fit in at normal temperatures. On cooling, the oversize ions are squeezed out and the crystal forms two distinct mineral species, usually intergrown in grains or layers; this process is known as *exsolution*.

LEFT Topaz (Villa Rica, Brazil)

CRYSTALS

The study of crystals can be quite difficult, but many minerals form crystals which are immediately recognisable in the field or under the microscope. Crystals get their shape from the way in which their atoms pack together – the packing is in turn dependent upon the chemical composition of the substance. While many crystals can be visually recognized with little difficulty it is harder to describe them precisely in words. The crystallographer postulates laws which are briefly reviewed here. We also look at the overall shape of crystals and at the terms used to describe them. Crystals react with light in a number of ways and these are discussed with a view to understanding some simple methods of identification.

Very large gypsum crystals can be found in the Cave of Swords, Naica, Mexico.

The best way to get used to describing mineral crystals is to examine as many as you can – in museum showcases or, even better, in the field. It is hard to represent three-dimensional objects on the two-dimensional page; the way in which atoms form crystals can be learned by using the ball-and-stick kits available from some laboratory suppliers and highly recommended.

Although crystals are not really very hard to understand, they are hard to describe as language is an inadequate tool to create three-dimensional pictures. A new language has to be learned in which common words like 'form' and 'habit' take on different and specific meanings from those in common usage. Crystals obey a number of simple laws and these are usually seen as immediately relevant to the specimen found in the field – for example, the law that states that interfacial angles on all examples of a mineral will be the same.

Human beings have always recognized and prized shiny stones with smooth faces. Transparent stones were endowed with magical or medicinal properties and rock crystal was once thought to be water frozen so hard that nothing could melt it. A Greek word, *krustallos*, was given to these objects and the name gradually came to apply to any mineral body with flat surfaces and a more or less regular shape.

Virtually all known substances are crystalline, apart from glass and the well-known gemstone opal. Crystals differ from these two substances in the arrangement of their atoms. In a crystal there is always a regular atomic structure, but this is not the case with glass or opal, which are known as amorphous or 'without form'. In most crystals

ABOVE *Muscovite (Brazil)*   BELOW *Opal (Australia)*

Rutilated quartz (Minas Gerais, Brazil)

there is no outward sign of this internal regularity which can only be detected by sophisticated techniques; although simple optical tests depend on crystalline properties, they do not show the details of the atomic arrangements. When a crystal shows a set of fine smooth faces, it has been able to grow in a favourable environment without interruption to the supply of the liquid from which it grows and without disruptive changes in temperature.

Crystals grow by the repetitive accretion of material to a mass which originated from a process known as nucleation. Some crystals grow from liquids, some from vapours and others from the solidification of molten material. Granites show crystals derived from melts: they are large specimens of quartz, feldspar and mica which formed as the molten rock cooled. Crystals grown from liquids include such simple examples as salt, which is dissolved by water at room temperature. Quartz, on the other hand, will not dissolve in water, except at temperatures and pressures well above those of the normal atmosphere. Crystals

vicinity of volcanoes, around the fumaroles (vents) by which the gases escape to the atmosphere. The crystals reach the solid state direct from the vapour. Sulphur crystals, often with many faces, are formed in this way.

Crystals must have a nucleus from which growth is initiated, and the size of the nucleus is critical. The most rapid growth occurs when the arrival of material on a surface creates suitable sites for fresh material to attach itself. Various types of dislocation – errors in the atomic arrangements which are by no means as perfect as one might expect – make some sites more suitable for the attachment of new material. Other types of accretion on a face are conditional upon the formation during growth on that face of steps or ledges. New material grows on these ledges.

The shape of the growing crystal is constantly modified by changes in the arrival of feed material. When fresh material accretes as layers of atoms on a face, that face grows fast in a direction at right angles to it. As more feed material arrives, the face becomes smaller. It can be compared to faces on each side. As the pyramid gets taller, the sloping faces get smaller and so does the upper surface, which ends in a point. Some faces, on which feed material is deposited faster than on their neighbours, finish up as points or edges. The faces that grow at the slowest rate remain till the end and are the best developed.

Crystal growth is fraught with hazards, however; a crystal growing from a solution will remove material from the solution nearest to it and thus make the solution weaker in that area. The weaker part of the solution is replenished from other parts and this will happen more easily at edges and corners than at the centres of faces. In this way edges and corners grow preferentially and this preferential growth may produce characteristic hollowed-out crystals known as hopper crystals; a good example of this is bismuth. Dendritic or tree-like crystals arise from rapid growth from solution.

Crystal growth can also be affected by the presence of impurities. Unless the atomic structure of the growing crystal can accommodate an impurity, foreign material will be pushed ahead of the growing face, hindering the supply of material to that face and thus slowing its growth. Some impurities may be incorporated within the crystal as inclusions; in gem minerals particularly these may indicate the origin of a specimen, even pinpointing the mine from which it came.

Kyanite (USSR)

Realgar (Washington, USA)

Whether a face is smooth or rough depends upon its growth history. Large faces tend to be rougher since they have had more time to be involved in growth accidents. Sometimes one face will grow over another, giving rise to the sceptre effect characteristic of some quartz specimens. These crystals tend to grow from the walls of cavities, allowing their points to obtain feed material more easily than their bases. Sometimes the material overgrowing another mineral may be a different species, as in quartz on calcite. Selective encrustation allows one mineral to coat alternate faces of another, as when hematite coats alternate faces of quartz. Old overgrowths may persist as phantoms when they themselves are overgrown. Again, quartz provides the best examples. Curved crystals – again of quartz – arise when different parts grow with different alignments; the final like a single individual. These are found in Alpine locations. Dolomite crystals may also show the same kind of curvature and have been called saddle crystals.

Many crystal faces show small pits whose shape gives a clue to the crystal's structure. The pits arise from changes in the growth environment which cause dissolution rather than faster growth. Pits on a ruby crystal are triangular and those on beryl hexagonal, indicating trigonal and hexagonal symmetry respectively.

The general shape of a crystal is called its habit. Types of habit commonly found include:

acicular (like a needle), as in rutile
capillary (hair-like), as in millerite
columnar, as in tourmaline or beryl
platy, as in mica
bladed, as in kyanite
tabular (flat), as in barite or corundum
dendritic (tree-like), as in native metals such as
   copper or silver
wedge-shaped, as in gypsum
spear-shaped, as in sphene or descloizite

Many minerals produce crystals which are said to be twinned. Twinned crystals are of several kinds but all appear to be more than one individual, whereas the reverse is the case. The separate parts may simply interpenetrate each other (interpenetrant twins) or the individuals may relate to each other across a twinning plane (a sheet of paper held in two praying hands would be such a plane). Such twins are called contact twins and are characteristic of spinel. Many twinned crystals can be spotted by the presence of re-entrant angles or by butterfly-like shapes.

Some twins may be repeated to give a complex twin; in the gem mineral chrysoberyl three orthorhombic crystals are so grouped that they give an overall hexagonal appearance (pseudo-hexagonal twinning) which sometimes can only be recognized by the presence of re-entrant angles. Lamellar twinning groups together many thin crystals in books – except that each crystal is reversed with respect to its neighbours. This can be seen in a number of minerals, including corundum and plagioclase feldspar.

Inclusions within minerals may be solid, liquid or gaseous. They are grouped into three types:

Rhodonite (Franklin, New Jersey, USA)

protogenetic inclusions are always mineral and exist before their host is formed; syngenetic inclusions are formed at the same time as the host and may be solid, liquid or gaseous; epigenetic inclusions are formed after the host is completed and may include cleavages, fractures and damage due to radioactivity.

Inclusions reveal a lot about how and when crystals grew. Randomly oriented rutile crystals in rock crystal show that the rutile was formed first. Quartz is generally a late former and tends to envelop other species. Mutual orientation of host and inclusions may give attractive optical effects; green fuchsite mica plates in rock crystal give a green spangled effect known as aventurescence; similar effects can be seen in the sunstone variety

Dioptase (Guchab, Namibia)

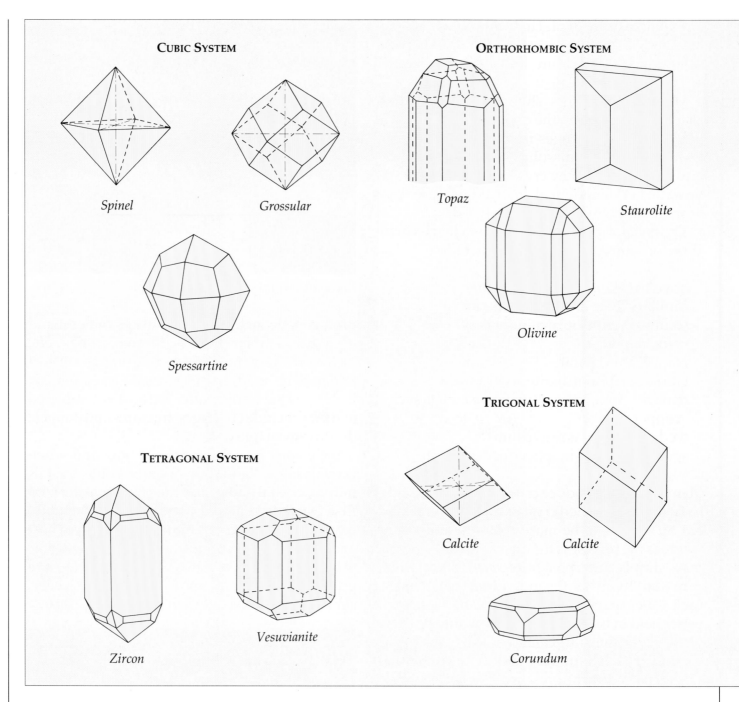

CUBIC SYSTEM

Spinel

Grossular

Spessartine

TETRAGONAL SYSTEM

Zircon

Vesuvianite

ORTHORHOMBIC SYSTEM

Topaz

Staurolite

Olivine

TRIGONAL SYSTEM

Calcite

Calcite

Corundum

of feldspar. Very small inclusions of crystals or channels arranged in parallel like thread on a reel show a line of light at right angles to their length. This is the cat's-eye effect (chatoyancy), best seen with very fine parallel inclusions in chrysoberyl. Asterism (a star effect) arises from inclusions of rutile in corundum, sometimes in other minerals. The star-like pattern is seen at right angles to an axis running through the crystal. In star quartz the effect is best seen by transmitted light and by reflected light in corundum. The rutile or other crystals arise from a process known as exsolution; they are randomly disseminated within the host and are precipitated out when the host is heated to the melting point of the included material but below its own melting point.

As time goes on, crystals change. They may slowly dissolve in water or acids, or they may transform to another related mineral. Realgar turns to orpiment when exposed for some time to air or a strong light. A crystal inside a rock may alter so that its chemical composition and structure change but its shape stays the same. Such crystals are called pseudomorphs and are common in quartz. Pseudomorphism also includes the replacement of organic material by silica, as in

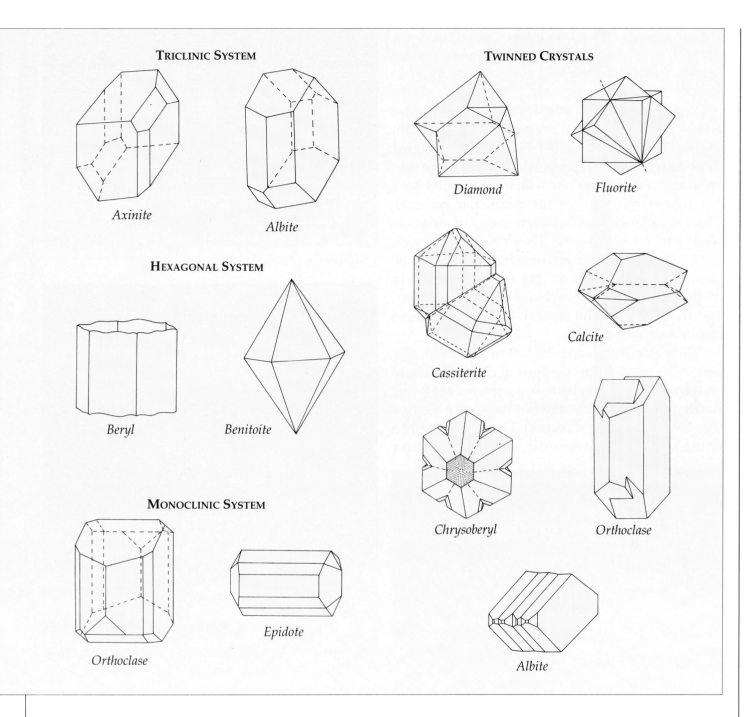

TRICLINIC SYSTEM

Axinite

Albite

HEXAGONAL SYSTEM

Beryl

Benitoite

MONOCLINIC SYSTEM

Orthoclase

Epidote

TWINNED CRYSTALS

Diamond

Fluorite

Cassiterite

Calcite

Chrysoberyl

Orthoclase

Albite

opalized wood or shell.

Many minerals do not occur as recognizable single crystals or groups but as masses with no characteristic external form. These masses are known as aggregates and are described by a number of different terms combined with their colour:

botryoidal (like a bunch of grapes)
reniform (kidney-shaped)
mamillary (breast-shaped)
globular or spherulitic (more or less spherical)

fibrous (consisting of long, thin crystals)
stalactitic (long crystals hanging down)
foliated or lamellar (sheets easily slit apart or like the pages in a book)
plumose (plume-like).
radiated or divergent (like a fan)
reticulated (net-like)
dendritic (tree- or plant-like)
arborescent (tree- or branch-like)

The characteristic appearance of a mineral's surface, as seen by reflected light, is known as its lustre. This may be described as adamantine, like a diamond, or sub-adamantine; silky, resinous, pearly (particularly of cleavage surfaces); vitreous (glassy – like most mineral surfaces); or dull (no lustre).

The regular internal atomic structure of a crystal allows it to have several properties which are not shared by amorphous substances. One of the most important of these properties is cleavage – a breaking along directions always parallel to a possible crystal face of the particular mineral. Cleavage planes pass between sheets of atoms in well-marked directions. This property is well shown by the mica group of minerals and can be classified: cleavage can be easy or difficult, distinct or poor. Perfect cleavage explains itself, and the nature of the surface left behind is also important.

When specimens are found in the field, the collector will look for the signs of cleavage. These include bands of spectrum (interference) colours. Parting is akin to cleavage but is usually along a significant twinning direction. There can be only a limited number of parting directions or planes in a

Chrysoberyl (Zimbabwe)

Beryl (USSR)

Malachite (Arizona, USA)

specimen, whereas cleavage can take place along an unlimited number of parallel planes. When a crystal breaks, rather than cleaving or parting, it is said to fracture, leaving an irregular surface behind. The type of fracture can help in identification; most minerals show a conchoidal or shell-like fracture, but other types of fracture may be even, uneven, hackly or splintery. These terms describe the type of surface remaining after fracture.

Crystals may show electrical properties. One of these is pyroelectricity, in which crystals become

Vesuvianite (Mexico)

electrically charged when heated and show the property by attracting dust. This is well shown by the gem mineral tourmaline.

As crystals are built up of atoms in a regular array, a number of features are able to assist mineralogists in testing. Steno published his researches on the angles between crystal faces, finding that for the same mineral these angles were the same. Between 1772 and 1782 Romé de l'Isle published similar findings as the Law of Constancy of Angles, which states that the angle between corresponding faces has a constant value for all crystals of a given substance. Similar major discoveries were made by the Abbé Haüy who first conceived the idea of building blocks stacking together to form a complete crystal. We now speak of these 'blocks' as unit cells which are the basic unit of the crystal's atomic pattern. This is repeated like the pattern might be on a three-dimensional wallpaper.

In 1912 Max von Laue discovered how crystals could diffract beams of X-rays, which led to the rays being used to identify minerals. Sheets of atoms in the crystal diffract X-rays at different angles when they are closely spaced rather than further apart, and when the diffracted rays strike a photographic film they form spots. The distances between the spots can be measured to give the atomic positions.

Atomic structures and crystal shapes obey the laws of symmetry and when we use this word

Sphalerite (Echigo, Japan)

Wulfenite (Arizona, USA)

about crystals we have to remember that crystals show three-dimensional symmetry. Simple, everyday objects show various kinds of symmetry – a cube rotated about an axis passing through the centre of one of its faces takes up a similar position in space four times in a complete rotation. The axis is thus one of four-fold symmetry.

An axis passing through the centre of one of the faces of a brick is one of two-fold symmetry since it presents the same aspect only twice in a complete rotation. Some crystals show reflection symmetry; as in left and right hands, one is the mirror image of the other. A centre of symmetry in a crystal has a corresponding face or edge on either side of it. A cube has a centre of symmetry while a pyramid has none. It is very important to remember that crystals found in the field only very rarely show

Barite (Oklahoma, USA)

Benitoite (California, USA)

Rhodochrosite (Colorado, USA)

the idealized symmetry of drawings in a book. This is because some faces develop more strongly than others. However, X-rays will show that the underlying symmetry is always present.

Crystals are assigned to seven systems which in turn can be divided into thirty-two classes. Even though the crystals belonging to a particular system vary a good deal in shape, they all show symmetry properties in common. The systems are conveniently distinguished from each other by their crystallographic axes, or axes of reference. These are imaginary straight lines parallel to actual or possible crystal edges. The cubic system has the highest symmetry and the triclinic system the lowest.

We can look at the different systems by considering the form shown by a crystal. The word form has a special meaning in crystallography; it means the assemblage of faces shown by a crystal which are dictated by its symmetry and which can identify the crystal even when only one or two faces are present. In the cubic system the cube and octahedron are characteristic forms. Open forms need another form to complete a crystal and closed forms are complete in themselves, as in cubes.

A crystal with four-fold symmetry may show prominent prism form; a prism is defined as an assemblage of faces meeting in parallel edges – like a pencil with a flat base and chopped off at the point, or a box with no bottom or top. The ends of such crystals may be terminated by pyramid

shapes or by flat faces known as pinacoids. Usually the pinacoid form consists of a pair of parallel faces but one can be replaced by a different termination. The basal pinacoid is often a direction of cleavage, as in topaz. The form known as a dome has faces which intersect the vertical axis of the crystal and one of the lateral axes but one is always parallel to the other lateral axis. Pyramid forms consist of groups of faces which will intersect all the crystal axes which may be produced where necessary. The general shape of a crystal arising from particular combinations of forms is called its habit. Cleavage can often reveal a form; for example, the mineral galena cleaves into cubes, and calcite into rhombohedra.

The cubic system has three crystallographic axes, all of equal length and intersecting at right

Amethyst (Vera Cruz, Mexico)

angles. Common forms are the cube and the octahedron; others include the 12-faced rhombic dodecahedron and the 24-faced icositetrahedron. Crystals, like many garnets, show combinations of forms by producing fine parallel grooves or striations between larger faces. Pyrite forms cubes, as do fluorite and galena; spinel and diamond are commonly found as octahedra. Tetrahedrite occurs as tetrahedra, with four identical faces of equilateral triangles. The tetragonal system has three crystallographic axes intersecting at right angles; two are the same length, while the third is longer or shorter. Rutile is found as tetragonal bipyramids (two pyramids joined base to base). Other tetragonal crystals show prismatic forms with varied terminations.

Other crystals of the tetragonal system include

Brazilianite (Minas Gerais, Brazil)

prismatic vesuvianite, bipyramids of scheelite and flat, square plates of wulfenite. In the hexagonal system there are four axes of reference, three equal in length and intersecting at 60 degrees; the fourth is at right angles to them and longer or shorter. Minerals like beryl form hexagonal prisms terminated by pyramids or pinacoids, and other minerals form hexagonal bipyramids. The rhombohedral class of the hexagonal system is now recognized as a system of its own, called trigonal. Prismatic crystals show three-fold rather than six-fold symmetry and a common form is the rhombohedron as shown by calcite. Quartz and tourmaline also belong to the trigonal system, which includes corundum as a gem-quality member. Minerals of the hexagonal and trigonal systems are hard to distinguish but surface markings give a clue to the six- or three-fold symmetry. At first sight unequal development of prism faces can make a trigonal crystal like a hexagonal one.

Crystals of the orthorhombic system are referred to axes which meet at right angles but which are of unequal length. Forms are prism,

pinacoid, pyramid and dome. Well-known examples include topaz, which forms prismatic crystals terminated by dome and pyramid forms at one end and by the basal pinacoid at the other; they show a rhombic cross-section. Barite shows a flattened (tabular) prismatic habit. Chrysoberyl shows characteristic pseudo-hexagonal twins.

The three crystallographic axes of the mono-clinic system are unequal in length. One axis is at right angles to the plane of the other two which do not meet at right angles. Prism and pinacoid are common forms. The mica minerals form platy

LEFT Proustite (Chile)

Vivianite (Oruro, Bolivia)

Tetrahedrite (Isère, France)

inside is called the refractive index of the crystal and this can be measured quite simply to give a valuable identification feature.

When there are two refracted rays, their velocities may differ considerably. Each has its own refractive index and the difference between them gives the birefringence of the specimen. In the case of transparent gem minerals a high birefringence will show by an apparent separating of the back facet edges when the stone is cut and viewed through the top or table facet. In addition, each of the two refracted rays is polarized in an opposite sense to the other. Polarized light vibrates in one direction only at right angles to the direction of travel of the ray; in unpolarized light vibration takes place in all directions at right angles to the direction of travel. This feature is also useful in identification when Polaroid cuts out one of the vibration directions. Where two pieces of Polaroid are so placed that all vibration directions are blocked they are said to be crossed and a mineral placed between them behaves in ways which can assist identification.

Many minerals owe their colour to a chemical impurity and others to elements which belong rightly to the particular species. Minerals coloured by elements which are a regular part of their chemical composition are said to be idiochromatic; those coloured by 'foreign' elements are called allochromatic. The gemstone peridot, a variety of the mineral olivine, a magnesium-iron silicate, owes its green colour to iron and is thus idiochromatic. Ruby, an aluminium oxide, is coloured by chromium and is thus allochromatic. The presence or absence of one of the colouring elements is not, however, always a factor in the colour of a mineral.

The colouring elements are numbers 22–29 on the periodic table of the elements: titanium, vanadium, chromium, manganese, iron, copper, nickel and cobalt. Titanium and iron combine to give blue in a number of minerals, including sapphire; vanadium gives green in beryl; chromium gives red in ruby and red spinel, green in emerald and jadeite; manganese gives a pinkish-orange in spessartine and rhodochrosite; iron gives a range of colours, the greens and reds being 'quieter' than those given by chromium – it also gives yellow in sapphire and blue in spinel; cobalt colours minerals pink and, very occasionally,

crystals in the monoclinic system and gypsum forms long or tabular prismatic crystals. The important families of the pyroxenes and amphiboles show prismatic cleavages, those in pyroxene meeting at nearly 90 degrees and those in amphibole meeting at about 124 degrees. The triclinic system has the lowest symmetry of all the systems. None of its crystallographic axes are the same length and they do not intersect at right angles.

Crystals and Light

Crystals and light interact in special ways which are of great service to the mineralogist. In this context amorphous substances behave in similar ways to crystals of the cubic crystal system. When the mineral is transparent, a ray of light will traverse it at a particular velocity from which it will have been slowed from its velocity in space by atoms of the crystal. This incident ray will be split into two in crystals which are not cubic and each refracted ray will travel at a different velocity as it passes through the crystal. The ratio between the velocity of the incident ray outside the crystal and

Scorodite (Mexico)

blue; nickel gives a bright apple green in the chrysoprase variety of quartz; and copper gives the blue of turquoise and the green of malachite.

When an appropriately cut mineral, such as diamond, gives flashes of spectrum colour, the effect is called dispersion. In opal the play of spectrum colour is due to diffraction from minute spheres of silica and the voids between them. Spectrum colours may also be seen when there is a crack or cleavage within a mineral or at its surface. This is due to components of the incident ray being retarded with respect to other components when crossing a thin film such as that provided by a thin crack. Some parts of the ray are cancelled out and others reinforced to give an effect of colour alternating with darkness. The colours are known as interference colours and are also seen on soap bubbles or oil slicks. The actual colours seen depend on the thickness of the film and the wavelength of the light.

When some minerals are placed in ultra-violet radiations or in X-rays they may give off a glow unlike that of their normal colour. The response is always of a higher wavelength than that of the stimulating radiation and the effect is known as luminescence or fluorescence. When the effect persists after removal of the stimulus, the glow is called phosphorescence. Ultra-violet radiation is either long- or short-wave (LWUV or SWUV). Similar effects are obtained with the more powerful X-rays. When a crystal changes colour when viewed from different directions, the effect is called pleochroism. Change of colour without change of direction has been called the alexandrite effect since this variety of chrysoberyl shows red in tungsten or candle light and green in daylight.

MINERALS OF VALUE TO MAN

Minerals do not only look attractive, many have uses as well. Minerals form gemstones, road and building stones, ores from which metals can be extracted, and fuels. We review the ways in which some minerals of economic importance are formed and how they are mined.

These sedimentary rocks from Israel show
characteristic bedding and contain gypsum.

Minerals have been used as tools, building materials, ornaments and weapons all through man's time on earth. Some have even had magical properties ascribed to them and many have been used in barter. Flint mines dating from Neolithic times can be found in chalk downs, but today the search for minerals is highly sophisticated, with remote sensing giving prospectors a powerful tool to supplement field investigation. An economic mineral deposit must contain useful minerals and be capable of being worked at a profit. This explains why a mine may be in full production one day and closed the next; the mineral produced may perhaps have dropped in price on the world's metal exchanges.

A desired element must exist in a concentration

Gold (California, USA)

high enough to make its extraction worth while. For example, panning for gold in the Witwatersrand area of South Africa is too primitive when the concentration of gold there is about 1,750 times the average for the earth's crust in general. Similarly, copper and zinc deposits in Namibia are 1,000 times the average, while lead is up to 10,000 times the concentration factor. There are ninety-two naturally occurring elements and eight of these constitute nearly ninety-nine per cent by weight of the earth's crust. Some elements are so dispersed through common minerals that they do not occur in major concentrations. This makes them expensive to extract.

The chemical composition of a mineral dictates whether it occurs native (that is, not combined with other elements), or whether it is found as oxides, carbonates, silicates, sulphides or other compounds. Aluminium has only one ore mineral, bauxite, a mixture of fine-grained hydrous aluminium oxides. However, it does occur in a large number of common minerals, although these cannot be worked for aluminium in any practical way. So, the working of an element depends on its local concentration and on the ease of its extraction from the ore.

Metals are the most important economic minerals. Metalliferous deposits consist of the ore (the mineral sought) with gangue (other unwanted minerals). The metal content of the ore is called its tenor. Some minerals which would once have been regarded as gangue are worked later on as techniques of recovery improve or the demand for the metal becomes insistent. Fluorite occurs with lead and zinc ores in north-east England; when the ores were worked out, the fluorite was then wanted as it had become important for the iron and steel industries. In some instances dumps are reworked, as well as veins in old mines.

Magmas (molten rocks) cool and solidify when they reach the surface. Heavy magmatic minerals may crystallize early and sink by gravity to the bottom of the magma chamber to give magmatic segregations at temperatures around 1,500 to 700°C. The Bushveld igneous complex in South Africa is a good example of this process and is worked for chromite and magnetite.

Materials with a low boiling point (volatiles) are not taken up by early-forming crystals. They concentrate in the fluids left after the first minerals have crystallized from them and there join other elements which do not easily enter minerals because of their atomic structures. These liquids enter cracks and fissures in the parent igneous rock or in the neighbouring country rock and there crystallize as high-temperature pegmatite bodies. Large crystals are characteristic of pegmatites, and the quartz, feldspar and mica of granite pegmatites are often worth working. As rare elements enter pegmatite formations, they are sought by collectors as a source of rare minerals; the lithium mineral spodumene is a good example. Granite pegmatites are also a source of the element beryllium.

Watery solutions left behind after the consolidation of magmatic material force themselves

Scheelite (South Korea)

Chalcocite (Montana, USA)

Stibnite (Kremnica, Czechoslovakia)

into adjacent country rocks to form hydrothermal mineral deposits. In the south-west mining area of Cornwall, England, granites are believed to have intruded 270 to 280 million years ago. Fluids associated with the crystallizing granite travelled upwards under pressure through fissures in the country rock. These fluids may have been the source of the metallic ore-forming elements, or these may have existed before the granite formed.

In this area ore and gangue minerals are found in a series of concentric zones. These zones can be related in depth and lateral extent to the three recognized divisions of hydrothermal deposits. Ore minerals which crystallize at the highest temperatures (in the hypothermal zone) are cassiterite, wolframite and scheelite. Their associated gangue minerals are tourmaline, fluorite, chlorite and hematite. At slightly lower temperatures a range of copper minerals crystallizes in the hypothermal zone, and at still lower temperatures in the mesothermal zone the minerals galena, sphalerite and argentite are formed with the gangue minerals fluorite, barite, dolomite and calcite. The lowest temperature (epithermal) zone provides the iron minerals siderite and hematite with stibnite, bournonite and tetrahedrite.

Much of this mining area is covered by gossan or 'iron hat'. This is a mixture of gangue minerals with iron and manganese oxides from which soluble minerals have been dissolved. They have been washed down and redeposited in lower enriched layers which contain azurite, malachite and cuprite. In turn this overlies a layer of secondary sulphide enrichment with the minerals bornite and chalcocite.

All the deposits mentioned above were formed in the earth's crust, sometimes at great depths, but now outcrop at or near the surface as a result of geological uplift and erosion. Other mineral deposits are formed by surface processes and contain minerals which have been concentrated by the sedimentary cycle of weathering, transport

Elbaite (Mesa Grande, California, USA)

Silver (Germany)

and sedimentation. Evaporite deposits, sedimentary rocks and residual deposits are characteristic of this group.

Evaporites are found in saline lakes and saline land-locked seas; they provide important gypsum, halite and salt deposits which arise as water evaporates from brine, leaving behind increasingly concentrated salts. The least soluble salts are deposited first and the more soluble ones later. Evaporites are also found where rivers and streams flow into enclosed inland lakes. Those streams crossing recent volcanic rocks may carry rare elements from the volcanic material, as well

Copper (Namibia)

as the commoner weathering products. Boron is typical of this kind of stream. Fossil fuels, oil and coal are formed by sedimentary processes from organic debris.

Sedimentary rocks are also economically important. Clays are used in ceramics and refractories, or as bricks and tiles. Sandstone is used in mortar or concrete, and quartz sand is used in the manufacture of glass. Gravels are used in aggregates for concrete. Some sedimentary rocks are used as ornamental building stone.

Residual deposits arise from the mechanical or chemical breakdown of rocks. Tin and gold deposits can be formed in this way and gem minerals can be obtained from residual material overlying unweathered parent rocks. Many iron ores have a residual origin. Primary iron ores, such as pyrite or siderite, may be weathered into more easily worked hydrated iron oxides. Impure iron oxides, such as goethite, hematite and limonite, can form by the weathering of primary iron minerals and then be deposited in sedimentary rocks to replace material already present, which is carried away in solution. The iron ores of Lake Superior started as sedimentary deposits of Precambrian seas. These deposits had their silica leached out so that a virtually pure iron oxide in the form of hematite

Siderite (Auvergne, France)

Fluorite (Illinois, USA)

was left. These deposits are worked by opencast methods.

Weathering, transport and sedimentation constantly redistribute elements at the surface of the earth. Native metals, like gold, or ores of metals, like cassiterite, become concentrated during the transport process and are deposited in river beds or on a shallow continental shelf. These are called placer deposits and were often panned in the famous gold rushes of North America and elsewhere. The best places were found to be below waterfalls or rapids.

The professional prospector deals more commonly with secondary minerals – those formed by the action of water on exposed primary ores, deposited by hydrothermal solutions or formed by the crystallization of a magma. The water

dissolves some components of the primary ore and then percolates downwards through the rocks, redepositing them as secondary minerals. When a mining operation begins, the bulk of the ore may be made up of secondary minerals. As the operation proceeds, however, the secondary minerals are replaced by the primary ore which is found at greater depths. Most high-grade ores have been identified by now and most of them have been worked.

The skill and experience of the mining engineer is now usually devoted to the location and working of bodies of lower grade ore. This has to be worked at a speed great, enough to allow for sufficient profits to be made. A suitable and profitable output might well need to be up to 100,000 tonnes of ore a day.

IDENTIFYING MINERALS

Many minerals can be identified in the field and this chapter describes some of the simple tests used. Collectors should bear in mind that some tests may damage valuable specimens, and where there is doubt over identity professional help should be sought. Visits to major collections allow collectors to become familiar with a wide variety of species.

This precariously-balanced rock gives its name to the location – Balanced Rock, Utah, USA. Wind has eroded the sandstone.

Although many minerals will need specialized identification in the laboratory, the collector can do quite a lot in the field or at home. One of the simplest tests is hardness, or the capacity of a mineral to resist abrasion by other materials. The scale devised by Friedrich Mohs in the nineteenth century is still in use. It is not a quantitative scale and gives only a relative idea of hardness, but when used with care it is very useful and simple to apply. The Mohs scale, with ten as the hardest, reads:

10	Diamond	5	Apatite
9	Corundum	4	Fluorite
8	Topaz	3	Calcite
7	Quartz	2	Gypsum
6	Orthoclase	1	Talc

The scale is diagnostic only for diamond; such everyday objects as a fingernail and a penknife blade have a hardness of 2.5 and 5.5 respectively. Many minerals show a variation in hardness with direction; kyanite is seven across the crystal length and four along it. In general, oxides and silicates are harder than sulphides, halides, borates, sulphates and phosphates. Native metals also tend to be soft. Many minerals, including the gem mineral opal, are unable to resist abrasion by airborne dust, which has a hardness of about seven. A majority of the important gem minerals are harder than seven.

Along with hardness, tenacity or toughness is also important for ornamental minerals. Jadeite and nephrite, the two jade minerals, are not particularly hard but are very tough due to

Calcite (Ohio, USA)

Fluorite (Cornwall, England)

minute, interlocking crystals making up their structure. Some minerals, like gold, are sectile in that they can be pared without powdering by the blade of a knife. Brittle specimens, like apatite or calcite, powder easily. When a mineral can be hammered without powdering, it is malleable; gold is an excellent example. When thin sections of a mineral can be bent without breaking, it is said to be flexible. When a bent piece springs back into shape, it is said to be elastic.

The streak of a mineral is the powder left behind when a specimen is firmly drawn across an unglazed porcelain streak plate. Many apparently dark minerals may give an unexpectedly light streak and this is a very useful field test. Hematite appears black in its massive state but gives a red streak and will also give a red powder. Many silicates and carbonates give a white streak. This test is perhaps most useful for the various oxides of iron.

The advantage of hardness and streak tests in the field is their simplicity and economy of equipment. Hardness can be tested with hardness pencils, in which sharp edges of standard minerals are set. The collector should observe the results of the test with a lens to ensure that a scratch has actually been made. It is easy to mistake the powder left by a scratch – it could come from the testing mineral rather than from the mineral being tested. In the case of minerals with an easy cleavage, streak and hardness tests should be applied with care.

Back at the bench a useful and easy test is to ascertain the specific gravity (SG) of a mineral. This is the ratio of the weight of a given volume of the mineral to the weight of an equal volume of water. Corundum, for example, weighs about four times as much as water since its SG is 3.99–4. The SG of diamond is 3.52 and of gold 19.3. Minerals with a high SG will feel heavier than they look when picked up; this is called 'hefting', but a more accurate test is to weigh the specimen, first in air, then submerged in water. In water the weight will be less than in air because of the

Gypsum (Oklahoma, USA)

upthrust of the water, which is equal to the weight of the water displaced by the specimen. This is the application of Archimedes' Principle. The formula can be written:

$$SG = {}^A\!/_{A-W}$$

where A is the weight of the specimen in air and W its weight in water. To be completely accurate, distilled water should be used and it should be free from bubbles. If another liquid is used, the figure obtained by the formula should be multiplied by the SG of that liquid (obtainable from tables).

When water is used, a drop or two of detergent should be added to reduce surface tension which can seriously affect results. This kind of test can only be carried out on relatively large, non-porous specimens. Smaller ones, particularly faceted gem stones, can be immersed in a series of liquids whose SG is known and their behaviour observed. Some will sink quickly, some will float on the surface and others (where the match is close) will

remain suspended when pushed beneath the surface with a glass rod. Here again, surface tension must be allowed for.

Care should be taken with the liquids which may have harmful effects on long exposure. Liquids in most common use are methylene iodide, with an SG of 3.3, and bromoform, with an SG of 2.8. These can be diluted with each other or with acetone. Those engaged in testing gemstones will keep sets of standard liquids diluted for convenience, with an 'indicator' suspended in each jar. The indicator may be a mineral of known SG or may be a piece of glass with the SG engraved upon it.

For minerals of an SG higher than 3.3, the liquid Clerici solution may be used. This is an aqueous solution of thallium formate and thallium malonate; highly poisonous, it should be used only by professionals, and as an aqueous solution it must be diluted with distilled water. Very large specimens may be immersed using a clean plastic dustbin as the water container.

Optical Examination of Specimens

The lens is perhaps the most valuable field companion. The best and most convenient magnification is 10x and all modern lenses are free from colour fringes and edge distortion. Keep the lens close to the eye and bring the specimen up to it. Most collectors will want a microscope sooner or later. The amount of magnification provided is less important than the availability of an adequate working distance (the space between specimen and lower lens). Generally, a magnification of 20x–40x will be enough to show up all major features of a specimen. When the specimen is transparent, the microscope may reveal characteristic and diagnostic inclusions which may in some cases indicate not only the species but the mine it came from. Details of inclusions will be found in standard texts on gemstones.

Specimens with high birefringence will appear to double ruled lines viewed through them on rotation. The refractometer will indicate the refractive index of a specimen provided it can give a face sufficiently flat to be tested. Details of the process will be found in mineralogical and gemmological texts. Pleochroism can be observed with the eye or via a simple instrument, the dichroscope. The spectroscope will show diagnostic spectra (dark vertical lines crossing a continuous coloured spectrum) when certain elements are present in a specimen.

Willemite (New Jersey, USA)

MINERAL DESCRIPTIONS

In this section minerals are described in traditional chemical order, as in most large museum collections and displays. Entries give chemical composition, hardness and specific gravity with notes on refractive index for some of the major gem species. We describe the mode of occurrence and give some of the major localities. The crystal system, form and habit are also given but, since so many minerals show considerable variation, we have only given the most characteristic examples.

The Grand Canyon of the Colorado River, USA, reveals many colours of rock along its walls. Layers of rock can clearly be seen.

If we were to give all the details by which the mineralogist distinguishes one mineral from another most of the following pages would be occupied by numerical data. These would be hard to interpret and in any case would be appropriate only for laboratory investigation of specimens. For simplicity and for the better understanding of specimens that can actually be seen without a microscope (hand specimens) the details given below are restricted to chemical composition, form, habit, hardness and specific gravity. For one or two minerals with gemstone application the refractive index is also given.

The hardness of a mineral is a useful field test and many minerals have a directional hardness which aids identification. Specific gravity can more easily be tested in the laboratory but the rough shape of a crystal may give some idea of its crystal system, form and habit even when first found. In the same way some minerals have a characteristic lustre (as that shown by diamond) that can help in identification. Characters depending on how light is reflected by the specimen or how it passes through it can only be determined after part of it has been cleaned and polished.

Though some of the most attractive minerals are found only in one or two places many of the rest occur widely over the surface of the earth. In these cases only the most important locations have been mentioned; for a more complete coverage readers will need to consult larger mineralogical texts or to look through state and country mineralogies, where they exist. It is, of course, always worth consulting the local Geological Survey which may exist on both national and state level in major countries. In addition to the localities where minerals may be found, concise information about how they are formed is also given here. The major rock types in which a particular species may occur are identified and some associated minerals are also mentioned where appropriate.

CHEMICAL CLASSIFICATION

We have seen in the chapter on mineral chemistry that an atom with an electrical charge is called an ion and that ions which lose electrons in the attempt to gain inert gas configuration are called cations while those which gain electrons in the same attempt are called anions. Cations are positively charged and anions negatively charged.

Many mineral collections are arranged in a chemical order based on simple or complex anions. In this book – as in most other mineralogical texts – the order follows in detail the (London, England) Natural History Museum's *Chemical Index of Minerals*. This begins with elements and goes on through the various compounds listing the minerals in the various classes – oxides, carbonates, silicates and the rest, grouping those with the same anion together. This is quite a convenient system though if you want to compare minerals with the same cation the anionic groups will have to be searched first. In this book we have examples of elements, sulphides, oxides, silicates and other mineral families.

Sulphides, which include many of the metallic ores, form in the presence of sulphur and absence of oxygen; carbonates contain the complex anion $(CO_3)^{2-}$ and to some extent reflect the former presence of simple marine organisms from which many carbonate-bearing rocks are formed. Oxides are minerals with oxygen as the sole anion; hydroxides have the complex anion (OH). These last are formed in general by oxides in rocks which are affected by the presence of water. Oxides which occur in many types of rock are generally hard; this is because in many oxides the cation is smaller than the oxygen anion and allows close-packing and dense minerals.

The most complicated minerals, the silicates, have the complex anion (SiO_4) where silicon combines with oxygen. This combination forms tetrahedra which can join together in several different ways. They can occur separately or as pairs, rings, chains, double chains, sheets or frameworks and the minerals thus have a wide variety of properties. Further details on mineral chemistry can be found in other mineralogical texts such as the present writer's *Encyclopedia of Minerals and Gemstones* (Orbis, 1976).

COPPER

Cu

A member of the cubic crystal system, copper takes a number of interesting and attractive forms, ranging from cubes, octahedra and dodecahedra to wirelike forms. Crystals are often twinned and the metal is highly malleable and ductile. The hardness is 2.5–3 and the specific gravity 8.95. The lustre is metallic and the streak a shining pale red. Copper is a good conductor of heat and electricity.

Copper is reddish-brown with light rose on fresh surfaces. It is often found to contain traces of silver and other metallic elements. Occurring most commonly in basic extrusive rocks, it is also found in contacts with these rocks by sedimentary rocks, and in cavities in basalts and in sandstones.

Fine crystals are found at various places in the USSR, including Sverdlovsk and Nizhne Tagilsk, and in the USA around the Quincy mine, Hancock, Michigan, and Bisbee, Arizona. Crystals are found at Rheinbreitbach, Germany, and Montecatini, Tuscany, Italy. Large amounts of copper are found on the Keeweenaw Peninsula, northern Michigan, USA, and here it forms a belt over 200 miles long. When oxidized, copper accumulates a film of cuprite, and secondary copper minerals develop as weathering proceeds.

Copper (Michigan, USA)

SILVER

Ag

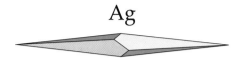

Silver is found in a wide variety of forms, including wires or scales and as cubic, octahedral or dodecahedral crystals of the cubic system. Crystals are commonly twinned. The hardness is 2.5–3 and the specific gravity 10.5. Silver is malleable and ductile and is silvery white with a grey or black tarnish.

Silver is found in the oxidation zone of ore deposits with other silver minerals; it also occurs in hydrothermal veins. Notable specimens come from Kongsberg in Norway, Freiberg, Aue and Mansfeld in Germany, Jachymov in Czechoslovakia, Huanchaca in Bolivia, the Quincy mine, Hancock, Michigan, USA, and from Juanxi, China. A number of localities in Mexico produce silver, particularly Chihuahua and Guanajuato.

Silver (Kongsberg, Norway)

GOLD

Au

Many people are familiar with gold in the form of nuggets but, as a visit to a mineral museum will show, this exceptional mineral also occurs in a variety of beautiful crystals. Although occurring in a variety of habits, crystals are very often twinned. Forms include cubes, octahedra and dodecahedra and it is commonly arborescent (tree-like), reticulated (net-like), filiform (as wires) or a sponge-like mass. There is no cleavage but the ductility and malleability of gold are highly characteristic. The hardness is 2.5–3 and specific gravity 19.3. When gold is pure it gives a golden streak; the lustre is metallic. It is frequently mixed with silver and sometimes copper (when it takes a reddish colour), platinum, lead, zinc or tin.

Gold is most commonly found in hydrothermal veins with pyrite and other sulphide minerals, and with quartz. It has also been reported from pegmatites and from contact metamorphic deposits. It also occurs, importantly, in hypothermal deposits and many of the world's major deposits are of this kind. In placer deposits gold is found as rounded or flattened grains or nuggets.

Some of the world's best-known gold deposits are at Cripple Creek, Colorado, USA (a shallow vein deposit), in the Transylvania area of Romania, where fine crystals are found in veins in or near volcanic vents, and in Siberia, where there are deposits near Sverdlovsk and placer deposits around Tomsk. Telluride ores in the Kalgoorlie area of Western Australia are highly important economically. Gold from the Witwatersrand district of the Transvaal, South Africa, is of the greatest importance.

Gold from Central and South America was more important in historical times than it is considered to be today, but in North America the placer deposits of Canada (and in particular deposits in the Klondike and the Yukon) and the mines of the United States are still producing gold. Important US deposits include the Comstock Lode in Nevada in addition to some

Gold (California, USA)

deposits in California and in a number of other states. The Californian deposits form part of the Mother Lode which extends for about 100 miles north from the Sierra Nevada. One or two occurrences of gold are occasionally worked in Wales, and it has also been reported from Heilongjiang and Guangxi, China.

DIAMOND

C

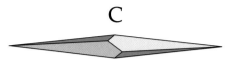

Diamond is for many the best-known mineral. Everyone knows a diamond when they see it, despite the many imitations on the market. It is still the hardest known substance, natural or synthetic, and its hardness, coupled with its remarkable optical properties, make it the ideal colourless faceted gemstone (sometimes yellow, pink, green or blue).

What is less well known is that diamonds, compared with other major gemstones, are not very rare. Although they are not as common as quartz or feldspar, enough are found each year to force producers to regulate availability and thus maintain prices worldwide. Therefore, to some extent, diamond is subject to the ebb and flow of market forces. However, falls in diamond prices are rare.

Diamond (Siberia, USSR)

Diamond is formed deep in the earth under conditions of great heat and pressure (such conditions have been reproduced in the laboratory to grow synthetic gem-quality diamonds). The actual details of formation are still unclear but crystals reach the surface through 'pipes' of a serpentinized olivine locally known as kimberlite. Crystals, in the form of octahedra, may be recovered by crushing the kimberlite or they may be found loose on the surface or in the beds of streams to which they have travelled after their host rock has weathered away.

Areas in which diamonds are found include South and West Africa, Brazil, India, Venezuela, Siberia and Australia. These countries are regular producers but occasionally diamonds have turned up in other places such as the United States. In general, major producers combine to maintain prices but inevitably a small proportion of their output arrives on the market through irregular channels. An effective black market has always operated and it is not always possible to say how the stone in your ring got there!

It is not difficult to recognize a diamond crystal, though opportunities to find one in the field are very limited. Crystals (of the cubic system) are usually octahedra or modified octahedra; many are twinned and some are flat with a glassy appearance. The surface looks rather greasy and, of course, it cannot be scratched. Crystals can be cleaved, however, and while this property is valuable for the polisher, it means that a fine specimen can be damaged if dropped or if one of its sharp points is used to scratch glass or other minerals. The flashes of colour seen in a well-cut brilliant are due to diamond's high dispersion, splitting up white light into its spectrum colours. A cut stone needs to be distinguished from imitations by an expert as there are now many different materials masquerading as the genuine article. Diamond is pure carbon (C); it has a specific gravity of 3.52 and a refractive index of 2.42.

GRAPHITE

C

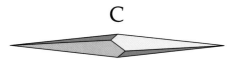

Graphite (Massachusetts, USA)

Graphite, with diamond, is one of the polymorphs of carbon but its appearance is quite unlike diamond's hard brightness. Graphite is a member of the hexagonal crystal system in which it forms fine foliated or leaf-like masses with a hardness of 1–2 and a perfect basal cleavage. The specific gravity is 2.1 and the lustre varies from metallic to dull. Graphite is flexible and sectile with a greasy feel; contact with it, as users of pencils know, stains the fingers.

Opaque masses are found in strongly metamorphosed rocks in many different parts of the world. There are large deposits at Pargas, Finland, and Kropfmühl, Bavaria in Germany. In the west in the United States there is a deposit at Ticonderoga, New York.

SULPHUR

S

Sulphur forms beautiful dipyramidal or tabular crystals of the orthorhombic system. Although the cleavages are indistinct, sulphur crystals need careful handling and storing as they are notably brittle and heat-sensitive. The hardness is 1.5–2.5 and the specific gravity 2.07. The lustre is characteristically resinous to greasy and the streak is white. The crystals are coloured a sulphur to straw yellow and are transparent to translucent.

Sulphur often occurs in volcanic regions as a result of volcanic action; it may be given off in the gases arising at fumaroles, as at Yellowstone, Wyoming, United States. It is commonly found in sedimentary rocks of the Tertiary era and is associated with gypsum and limestone. All collectors know the magnificent sulphur crystals found on Sicily, mainly near Agrigento, in association with celestine, calcite, aragonite and gypsum. Sulphur is found in many other places in the world but these deposits furnish virtually all specimen material. The heat produced by the hand when sulphur is held may well cause it to crack.

Sulphur (Agrigento, Sicily)

CHALCOPYRITE

CuFeS$_2$

Chalcopyrite (Colorado, USA)

Chalcopyrite is an important ore of copper and the most common copper-bearing mineral. It is a member of the tetragonal crystal system in which it forms tetrahedra or botryoidal or reniform masses. Twinning is common; the hardness is 3.5–4 and the specific gravity 4.2. Chalcopyrite, with a metallic and sometimes iridescent appearance from its tarnish, is usually brassy-yellow in colour with a greenish-black streak.

Many sulphide ore deposits contain at least some chalcopyrite but most is carried in mesothermal and hypothermal veins which are the source of economic copper recovery. Pyrite is associated with chalcopyrite in hypothermal deposits with some tourmaline and quartz.

Intergrowths of chalcopyrite and other minerals are common, particularly sphalerite and tetrahedrite. It occurs on crystals of galena and sphalerite. Fine crystals are found in the Freiberg area of Saxony in Germany, and in the tin veins of Cornwall, England, especially at Camborne and the New Kitty mine, St Agnes. Crystals are also found at Ste Marie aux Mines, Alsace, France, at Kitzbühel, Tirol, and Hüttenberg, Carinthia, Austria, at Rio Tinto, Spain, at Campione, Grosseto, Italy, and at Ergani-Maden, Turkey. Fine crystal groups are found in Japan at Ani and Arakawa in Ugo province. Very fine crystals are found at the French Creek mines, Chester county, Pennsylvania, USA.

SPHALERITE

(Zn,Fe)S

Sphalerite, or zinc blende as it is sometimes known, forms crystals in the cubic crystal system. Forms include tetrahedra and dodecahedra and often show considerable complexity. Cleavable masses are common and single crystals show six directions of cleavage with a hardness of 3.5. Twinning is common; the specific gravity is 3.9–4.1. Sphalerite shows a variety of shades, ranging from colourless through yellow, green, brown, orange and red. It has a high dispersion and faceted stones show a play of spectrum colour rivalling that shown by diamond. Some specimens may show triboluminescence or an orange fluorescence under ultra-violet radiation. The streak is pale brown to colourless and the mineral is transparent to opaque. Sphalerite has a near adamantine lustre. The relatively few cut stones have a refractive index of about 2.40.

Sphalerite is the commonest ore of zinc and is found with galena and other sulphides in limestones, dolomites and other sedimentary rocks; it is also known from hydrothermal ore veins. Fine crystals come from Picos de Europa, Santander in Spain, Anneberg and Saxberget in Sweden, Príbram in Czechoslovakia, Mies in Yugoslavia, and Campione, Grosseto in Italy. In Germany it is also found in sedimentary rocks near Meggen, Westphalia, and in metamorphic deposits at Rammelsberg.

Other deposits occur at Franklin, New Jersey, and minute, ruby-coloured crystals are found at Joplin, Missouri. Recently clear, dark green crystals were found at the Iron Cap mine, Graham county, Arizona, USA. Additionally from the USA red material comes from Tiffin, Ohio. Black crystals occur in England at Alston Moor, Cumbria, and at various places in Cornwall, including St Agnes. It has been reported from Hunan and Guangxi, China. Fine green transparent material is found at Cananea, Sonora, Mexico.

Sphalerite (Arizona, USA)

CINNABAR

HgS

The scarlet sulphide of mercury, cinnabar, usually forms masses, but rhombohedral or thick tabular crystals with a perfect cleavage are also found. Twinning is frequent. The crystal system is trigonal and the hardness is 2–2.5. The specific gravity is 8.09; as well as scarlet, cinnabar may be brownish-red to lead grey. It may be transparent in thin pieces and stones have even been faceted. The material shows an adamantine lustre inclining to metallic, but becomes dull in friable pieces. Specimens may be slightly sectile.

Cinnabar is commonly found in veins near recently formed volcanic rocks and is the chief ore of mercury. Minerals found in association include pyrite, marcasite and stibnite. It is also found near hot-spring deposits and is thought to be deposited by alkaline solutions. Deposits in limestone in Turkestan have long been worked for mercury and the mineral is also found in schists in that area. Fine crystals are found at Mount Avala near Belgrade, Yugoslavia. Economically, the most valuable deposits are at Almaden, Ciudad Real, Spain. New Almaden, California, USA, also produces some cinnabar. Other deposits occur at Obermoschel, Germany, Glatschach, Austria, Santa Barbara, Peru, and Monte Amiata, Tuscany, Italy. There are several deposits in China, especially the Yanwuping mine, Wanshan county.

Cinnabar (China)

GALENA

PbS

Galena (Oklahoma, USA)

Galena is one of the metallic ores which occurs in recognizable crystals; the familiar cubes, often modified to octahedra or forming combinations of cube and octahedron and showing a metallic lustre of shining black, can be found in a great number of situations. Galena has a perfect cubic cleavage and a hardness of 2.5–2.75. The specific gravity is 7.6 and the streak a lead grey. Some galena forms fibrous skeletal crystals and twinning is common.

Galena is the most important lead-bearing mineral and one of the commonest of the sulphides. It may occur in widely differing types of deposit, from sedimentary rocks to pegmatites; it occurs in hydrothermal ore veins and in contact metamorphic deposits. Deposits are found all over the world, with interesting crystals coming from Clausthal and St Andreasberg in Germany, the northern limestone Alps, Iglesias in Sardinia, Leadhills in Scotland, the Herodsfoot mine, Lanreath and Wheal Hope, Cornwall, England, and the Joplin district, Missouri, USA.

REALGAR

AsS

Realgar (Nevada, USA)

Realgar forms short prismatic crystals, often twinned, in the monoclinic crystal system. There is a perfect cleavage and the hardness is 1.5–2. The specific gravity is 3.56 and the colour red to orange-yellow. The lustre is resinous to greasy and the streak orange to red. Realgar is decomposed by HNO_3 and by long exposure to light; it is sectile and transparent to translucent. Realgar is found in low-temperature hydrothermal veins associated with lead and silver ores. Fine crystals, some of gem quality, are found in the USA at the Reward mine, King county, Washington, and at the Getchell mine, Nevada; in cavities with good crystals also from Mercur, Tooele county, Utah. In Europe deposits are found at Felsobanya and Nagyag, Romania, and in the Binntal, Valais in Switzerland. Finds also occur at Tajowa in Czechoslovakia, at Vesuvius, Solfatura and Cetine, Siena in Italy, Emet in Turkey, and Matra in Corsica. Fine crystals come from Rollenberg bei Bruchsal, Baden-Wurttemberg, Germany. Very fine crystals are reported from Hunan, China.

ORPIMENT

As_2S_3

Orpiment forms orange, yellow or brown prismatic crystals, or flaky masses of the monoclinic system with a hardness of 1.5–2 and a perfect micaceous cleavage. The specific gravity is 3.4–3.5 and the lustre is resinous to pearly. Although inelastic, orpiment is sectile and flexible; it is translucent to transparent.

Orpiment occurs as a low-temperature mineral in hydrothermal veins or as a hot spring deposit. It occurs as an alteration product of other arsenic minerals, particularly of realgar. It may be found as a sublimation product at fumaroles or as a product of mine fires.

In the USA fine, large crystals come from Mercur, Tooele county, Utah, and rich masses from the Getchell gold mine dumps, Nevada. It is found in the French Maritime Alps at Luceram and Duranus, and in Romania at Felsobanya and Kapnik. It occurs with realgar in the Binntal, Valais, Switzerland, at Jozankei, Hokkaido in Japan, Tajowa in Hungary, and from places in the southern Caucasus, USSR.

Orpiment (Peru)

STIBNITE

$$Sb_2S_3$$

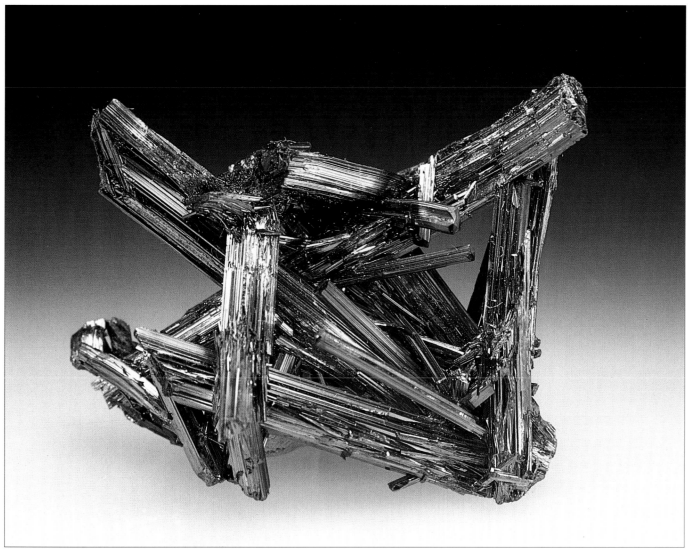

Stibnite (China)

Lead-grey, slender prismatic crystals of stibnite are sought by collectors who are particularly interested in crystal groups from the mines at Ichinokawa, Japan. Stibnite crystallizes in the orthorhombic crystal system with a perfect cleavage and a hardness of 2. The specific gravity is 4.6 and the lustre is metallic, splendent on cleavage surfaces. The streak is lead- to steel-grey. Stibnite is slightly sectile and soluble in HCl. There is a blackish tarnish with some iridescence. Stibnite is the chief ore of antimony and occurs in low-temperature hydrothermal veins and in hot springs.

As well as the Japanese deposit mentioned above, stibnite is found in limestones at Pereta, Tuscany in Italy, and at Lubilhac, Haute Loire in France. It is also found at Wolfsburg, Harz in Germany, Felsobanya in Romania, where it forms radiating aggregates with barite, Lesnica in Yugoslavia, and at Wheal Boys, St Endellion, Cornwall in England. Stibnite is found in Idaho and several other states in the USA.

MOLYBDENITE

$$MoS_2$$

Molybdenite is the major ore of molybdenum and is found worldwide. It forms thick or thin tabular or barrel-like prismatic crystals in the hexagonal system; it is more commonly found as scales or as foliate masses. It has a perfect cleavage and is sectile. The hardness is 1–1.5 and the specific gravity 4.62–5.06. The colour is lead grey with a greenish streak. The lustre is metallic and the mineral has a greasy feel. Molybdenite occurs as an important deposit at the Climax mine, Lake county, Colorado, USA. It also occurs at the Knaben mine in Norway, at Cinovec in Czecho-slovakia, Bleiberg, Carinthia in Austria, and at Radautal bei Bad Harzburg in Germany.

Molybdenite (Namibia)

PYRRHOTITE

$$Fe_{1-X}S$$

Pyrrhotite crystallizes in the monoclinic and hexagonal systems, forming tabular or platy crystals, or steeply pyramidal crystals with horizontally striated faces. The hardness is 3.5–4.5 and the specific gravity 4.7. The colour is bronze-yellow to brown and the lustre metallic. The streak is dark greyish-black. Tarnishing gives iridescence and the mineral shows magnetism of varying intensity. Pyrrhotite is found chiefly in basic igneous rocks with other sulphides. Fine large crystals are found at Kisbanya, Transylvania in Romania, and Val Passiria, Trentino in Italy. The Morro Velho gold mine in the state of Minas Gerais, Brazil, provides very large crystals. Deposits can be found in a number of places in the western United States, as well as at Kongsberg in Norway, in the Siegerland and from St Andreasberg in Germany, and at Trepca, Yugoslavia. Large, well-formed crystals come from the San Antonio mine, Aquiles Serdan, Chihuahua, Mexico.

Pyrrhotite (Uri, Switzerland)

PYRITE

FeS$_2$

Pyrite (Elba, Italy)

Bright brassy crystals and crystal groups of pyrite are in every mineral collection. They pose problems of storage and conservation but with care and the appropriate storage conditions (glass cabinets without wood are best) they will make a fine display. Pyrite is a member of the cubic crystal system in which it forms cubes or pyritohedra with various other forms; some crystals may be twinned. The hardness is 6–6.5 and the specific gravity 5. The metallic lustre and brass-yellow colour are easy to recognize; some iridescence occurs as tarnish develops and the streak is greenish-black or brownish-black. When struck with steel, pyrite may emit sparks and it is a conductor of electricity.

Pyrite is the most abundant of the sulphides and can be found worldwide and in almost every type of environment. It occurs in moderate to high-temperature hydrothermal deposits. Large bodies may be found in contact metamorphic deposits and in sulphide veins. It may occur as concretions in sedimentary rocks and may partially replace organic fossil material. Some fine crystals can be found in metamorphosed sediments. Fine crystals may be found in a very large number of places. Some of the best-known examples come from the Freiberg area of Germany and from the St Gotthard Pass, Switzerland. Exceptionally fine, large crystals come from the island of Elba in association with hematite. Fine pyritohedra are found at Traversella, Piedmont in Italy, and at places in France, including Saint-Pierre-de-Mésage, Isère, and at Arnave, where it occurs as octahedral crystals in limestone. In England pyritized fossils are found at Lyme Regis, Dorset, and crystals occur at Liskeard and St Just, Cornwall. Cubic crystals are found in a chlorite schist at Chester, Vermont, USA.

MARCASITE

FeS$_2$

Marcasite (Missouri, USA)

The term marcasite is used by some jewellers for an ornamental material which is the mineralogist's pyrite. Marcasite is a mineral in its own right and forms tabular or pyramidal crystals in the orthorhombic system. The hardness is 6–6.5 and the specific gravity 4.8–4.9. Marcasite is less stable than pyrite. The name 'cockscomb pyrite' is given to aggregates of flattened, twinned crystals. The colour is a pale brass-yellow and some iridescence may be shown. The lustre is metallic. Some crystals show curved faces: the streak is greenish-black.

Marcasite is formed at low temperatures, usually in sedimentary environments or in low temperature veins. It occurs all over the world but notable occurrences are found at Príbram in Czechoslovakia, Saxony in Germany and Joplin, Missouri in the United States.

PROUSTITE

Ag$_3$AsS$_3$

To many collectors the deep red crystals of proustite are among the most desirable of minerals. They need to be stored away from bright light as they may develop a surface tarnish.

Proustite crystallizes in the trigonal system, forming rhombohedral or short prismatic crystals or masses. There is a distinct cleavage; the hardness is 2–2.5 and the specific gravity 5.6. The lustre is adamantine and the streak vermilion. Proustite is usually translucent but some pieces have been found which are transparent in thin sections. Proustite occurs in most silver deposits. The finest crystals reportedly come from the upper portions of vein deposits where they are recovered from vugs.

Very fine crystals were found at mines in Saxony, Germany, especially from the Freiberg area and the Himmelsfurst mine. Fine crystals associated with tetrahedrite, quartz and calcite come from Ste Marie aux Mines, Alsace, France. Perhaps the finest crystals of all are those from the silver deposits at Chanarcillo, Chile. These crystals may be up to 75 mm (3 in) long and are twinned.

OPPOSITE PAGE Proustite (Germany)

PYRARGYRITE

$$Ag_3SbS_3$$

Pyrargyrite usually occurs as deep red masses but may also form prismatic or scalenohedral crystals of the trigonal system. The hardness is 2.5 and there is a distinct rhombohedral cleavage. The lustre is adamantine to submetallic and the specific gravity is 5.85. There is a dark red streak.

This mineral is found in low-temperature hydrothermal vein deposits with other sulpho-salts and with silver. Very fine crystals come from the Harz area of Germany, Príbram in Czechoslovakia, Hiendelaencina in Spain, Montevecchio, Sardinia in Italy, Teufelsgrund, Munstertal in Germany, and Ste Marie aux Mines, Alsace, and Chalanches, Isère, France. It is also found at the Valenciana mine, Guanajuato, Mexico. Pyrargyrite is an important ore of silver.

Pyrargyrite (Saxony, Germany)

BOURNONITE

$PbCuSbS_3$

Bournonite (Ireland)

Bournonite is associated with the 'cog-wheel' crystals found in Cornwall, though they also occur in many other locations. Crystals, members of the orthorhombic system, are black to greyish-black and the cog-wheel form is caused by twinning. They have a hardness of 2.5–3 and a specific gravity of 5.8–5.9. There is a good cleavage in one direction and the lustre is metallic to adamantine.

Bournonite is a mineral of hydrothermal veins and moderate temperatures. It is associated with galena, sphalerite, pyrite, siderite, quartz and other minerals; indeed, it is sometimes found on galena. In England the finest crystals come from the Herodsfoot mine near Liskeard, Cornwall, and from mines in the St Endellion area, the latter giving rise to its early name, endellionite. Bournonite is also found at several locations in the Harz mountains of central Germany, especially around Neudorf. The mineral is also found in Romania, at Felsobanya and Nagyag, where it occurs with rhodochrosite.

There are also several deposits in Spain and Italy, and it is common in the tin veins of Bolivia. Good crystals are found at the Chichubu mine in the Saitama Prefecture, Japan, and at Broken Hill in New South Wales, Australia. Large crystals are found with siderite and sphalerite at Park City, Utah, and there is another US deposit at Cerro Gordo, Inyo county, California.

$$Cu_2O$$

Cuprite (Namibia)

Superb red crystals of cuprite are found in a number of places, some of facetable quality coming from the Onganja mine, Namibia. Cuprite belongs to the cubic crystal system in which it forms octahedra and sometimes dodecahedra or cubes; massive and earthy varieties are also found. The hardness is 3.5–4 and the specific gravity 6.14. Cuprite shows a metallic or adamantine lustre and gives a red streak, which may vary in shade, usually inclining to brown. Many crystals of cuprite develop a coating of green malachite – a particular characteristic of crystals from Namibia. Cuprite in turn may be found coating native copper.

It is found in the oxidized zones of copper ore deposits in association with malachite and with other copper minerals. A hair-like variety, chalcotrichite, is found at the Fowey Consols mine, St Blazey, and brilliant red crystals occur at the Phoenix mine, Linkinhorne, Cornwall, England. Chalcotrichite is also found at Leogang, Salzburg, Austria, and Rheinbreitbach, Germany. Fine crystals are found at Bisbee, Arizona, USA, and at several places in the Urals, USSR.

CHRYSOBERYL

$BeAl_2O_4$

This hard and attractive mineral gives us the gem stones alexandrite, cat's-eye and a fine, transparent yellow-green stone which has long been popular for ornamental purposes. The fortunate collector – who will have to go to Brazil or the Urals – will find that the orthorhombic crystals are twinned to give an overall hexagonal appearance. Virtually all specimens are found in alluvial gravels.

Alexandrite is famous for changing colour, from red in candlelight or tungsten light to green in daylight or fluorescent light. The two colours are not always very bright and the change is not peculiar to this mineral, but this quality is enough to make it desirable for collectors. The cat's-eye at its best has a translucent, honey-coloured background against which the 'eye' shows as a sharp blue-white line of light. Chrysoberyl has a hardness of over 8, specific gravity about 3.74 and a refractive index of 1.74–1.75.

Chrysoberyl (Brazil)

SPINEL

$MgAl_2O_4$

Spinel (New Jersey, USA)

The red spinel is a beautiful orange-red gem mineral which, like ruby, owes its colour to chromium. It is found in association with ruby in metamorphosed limestones or dolomites, or in alluvial deposits resulting from the breakdown of its original host. Blue spinel does not have quite the same blue as sapphire but rare cobalt-bearing varieties are a bright blue. So far these have been found only in Sri Lanka. Red spinel comes from Sri Lanka, Burma or Pakistan. The spinels belong to the cubic crystal system and are found as octahedra which are often twinned to give a butterfly shape. They are hard, at 8 plus on Mohs' scale, and have a specific gravity of 3.60 and refractive index of 1.72. Synthetic spinels are made to imitate other gemstones rather than spinel itself.

ZINCITE

(Zn,Mn)O

Zincite crystallizes in the hexagonal system, forming bipyramidal crystals terminated at one end (hemimorphic). Twinning is common and there is a perfect cleavage. The hardness is 4 and the specific gravity 5.6. Zincite is orange-yellow to deep red as a result of its manganese content; some transparent pieces have been cut as gem-stones but these are extremely rare. The lustre is sub-adamantine and the streak orange-yellow. Zincite of specimen quality is found only at Franklin, New Jersey, USA, where it occurs in the granular ore. This is cut by calcite veins in which the crystals are found. Spheres with willemite and calcite make attractive fluorescent specimens.

Zincite (New Jersey, USA)

CORUNDUM

Al_2O_3

Corundum (Mogok, Burma)

Although all rubies are red, not all sapphires are blue. Both are varieties of the mineral family corundum. The word sapphire can be used for specimens of any colour other than red, and in fact the corundum family does produce a wide variety of colours. The finest rubies can be the most expensive of the gem minerals as they are geologically rarer than diamond. Such rubies come almost invariably from Burma; ruby from other sources, though often very beautiful, is never quite the 'pigeon's blood' colour of the classic Burmese material. Other ruby-producing areas include Sri Lanka, whose rubies incline to pink, Thailand, Pakistan and some East African countries. Indian rubies tend to be dark and heavily included.

In recent years it has been found possible to improve the colour of some rubies, and though stones so treated can be detected, the trade is uncertain about their commercial standing. More serious, though long known, is the large-scale manufacture of synthetic rubies by a variety of processes. Distinguishing them from the genuine article is a task for the gemmologist. Corundum has a hardness of 9 and a specific gravity of 3.99. The refractive index is 1.76–1.77.

The colour of ruby is caused by the presence of a small amount of chromium. Crystals, members of the trigonal system, take the form of tabular prisms or rounded bipyramids, though many occur as water-worn pebbles. It is rare for them to be found in their parent rock, but ruby crystals have been noted in the rocks of north Pakistan. The rock in which they are formed is a metamorphosed limestone or dolomite, which is not very resistant to weathering.

Sapphires are found in a similar environment and largely from the same countries. The variety of colours in which they occur – blue, yellow, pink and dark green – is caused by the presence of iron. The brighter the colour, the more desirable a specimen will be as a gemstone.

QUARTZ

SiO_2

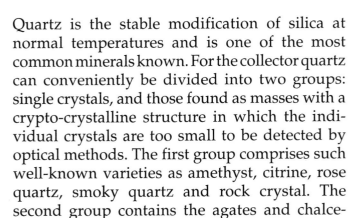

Quartz is the stable modification of silica at normal temperatures and is one of the most common minerals known. For the collector quartz can conveniently be divided into two groups: single crystals, and those found as masses with a crypto-crystalline structure in which the individual crystals are too small to be detected by optical methods. The first group comprises such well-known varieties as amethyst, citrine, rose quartz, smoky quartz and rock crystal. The second group contains the agates and chalcedonies, jasper, chrysoprase and carnelian.

Quartz crystallizes in the trigonal system, forming prismatic crystals terminated by pyramid-like rhombohedra. The prism faces are horizontally striated and many, if not all, crystals are twinned, although this may not be apparent from their external appearance. Quartz crystals may also display enantiomorphism – left- or right-handedness – and this can be detected by the position of small faces. Quartz is piezoelectric in that it develops an electrical charge under pressure and vice versa. This property is utilized on a large scale in the electronics industry.

Quartz has little cleavage. It is standard 7 on Mohs' scale. The specific gravity is 2.65 and the lustre is vitreous. The refractive index is 1.544–1.533. The amethyst and citrine varieties are violet to reddish-purple and orange-yellow to brown respectively, while smoky quartz is a characteristic greyish-brown, not unattractive. These varieties are found in a wide range of environments and in many countries. Colourless transparent quartz is called rock crystal.

Commercially the best material comes from Brazil, but fine crystals occur in Alpine deposits. Single crystals of rose quartz are uncommon but not excessively rare. The crypto-crystalline quartzes are also found all over the world in a variety of geological environments. Commercial material may be found on beaches. Chrysoprase is probably the rarest member of this group, owing

Quartz (Arkansas, USA)

its bright apple-green colour to the presence of nickel. It is found in Australia and Poland. Agates are banded, the bands often being enhanced by dyeing; onyx is usually black, frequently striped with white. Jasper is a dark-coloured beach pebble and carnelian is flesh-coloured.

Moss agate is usually yellowish with included mineral oxides giving a plant-like appearance. Fire agate gives a play of extraordinarily beautiful colour. Quartz frequently replaces organic material such as wood and silicified dinosaur bone takes a good polish.

OPAL

$$SiO_{2+}nH_2O$$

Opal is the only gem mineral which is amorphous, that is without the regular internal atomic structure which makes up a crystal. Opal therefore belongs to no crystal system, has no cleavage and cannot show any optical directional properties. The composition of opal varies with the water content and many authorities advocate storing it away from too much heat and dryness. Opal is porous and should never be placed in coloured liquids; if it has to be placed in a liquid for testing purposes, distilled water should be used.

Opal has a hardness of about 6.5 and a specific gravity of 2.1. Diffraction from regular three-dimensional spheroids and voids forming an array causes the play of spectrum colour. There are many varieties of opal and names have been given to hundreds of colour effects. In general, the chief classes are: black opal, where the play of colour is seen against a black or dark background; white opal, where the background is light or white; fire opal, with a red, yellow or orange body colour, sometimes with play of colour as well; and water opal, in which the play of colour appears almost to hang inside a transparent medium. Most opal is translucent.

The finest opal (black and white) comes from Australia, where the Lightning Ridge area of New South Wales produces the world's outstanding black opal specimens. Other major Australian locations are Coober Pedy and Andamooka, South Australia, and White Cliffs, New South Wales. Opal replacing wood is found in Nevada, USA. Mexico provides most of the fire and water opal. There are opal deposits in several other countries, including Brazil, which is becoming a commercial producer. Opal usually occurs in sandstone rocks as veins; some of these opals are so thin that they can only be sold with a backing. It is in this way that composite opals are made. Some fire opal is found in rhyolite.

Opal (Nevada, USA)

RUTILE

TiO$_2$

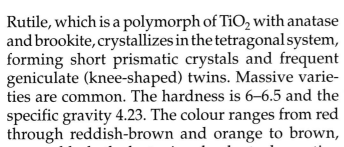

Rutile, which is a polymorph of TiO$_2$ with anatase and brookite, crystallizes in the tetragonal system, forming short prismatic crystals and frequent geniculate (knee-shaped) twins. Massive varieties are common. The hardness is 6–6.5 and the specific gravity 4.23. The colour ranges from red through reddish-brown and orange to brown, grey or black; the lustre is splendent adamantine and the streak pale yellow to brown. The mineral is translucent to transparent.

Rutile is characteristic of Alpine locations, where it occurs with quartz. Some rock crystal is filled with golden, hair-like rutile crystals and has been referred to as Venus' hair stone. The Alpine material forms in hydrothermal veins. It is found in the Binntal, Urserental and Tavetsch areas of Switzerland, and in the Austrian Zillertal at Saurüssel. It has also been found in pegmatite at Kragerö, Norway. It occurs at Magnet Cove, Arkansas and as fine large crystals at Graves Mountain, Georgia, USA. It also occurs in sands at a number of differing places in New South Wales, Australia and in Brazil. Rutile has a worldwide distribution.

Rutile in quartz (Minas Gerais, Brazil)

ANATASE

TiO$_2$

With rutile and brookite, anatase is a polymorph of titanium dioxide (polymorphs have the same chemical composition but different structures). Anatase is a member of the tetragonal crystal system and forms acute-angled pyramidal crystals which often form coatings on rock crystal. There is a perfect cleavage; the hardness is 5.5–6 and the specific gravity 3.9. Anatase has a metallic lustre and the colour ranges from brown or reddish-brown to indigo or black. The streak is colourless or pale yellow.

Anatase is characteristically found in Alpine-type deposits and is found as fine crystals in the Swiss Alps, notably from Santa Brigitta in the Tavetsch, Graubunden. In the Austrian Alps anatase is found in the Zillertal and elsewhere in the Tirol. Fine bluish-grey crystals on rock crystal come from a number of Norwegian localities, and blue crystals are found at Beaver Creek, Gunnison county, Colorado, USA. It has been reported from the Brazilian gem gravels. Generally, though, anatase occurs worldwide.

Anatase (Switzerland)

CASSITERITE

SnO_2

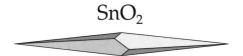

Cassiterite is the principal ore of tin and is found as crystals of the tetragonal system or as concretionary masses (wood tin). Crystals show short prismatic form and are often twinned. The hardness is 6–7 and the specific gravity 6.9. The lustre is adamantine to metallic and the colour ranges from near colourless through yellow to reddish-brown and black. The streak may be white, grey or brown. Rare faceted stones show a high dispersion.

Cassiterite is found chiefly in high-temperature hydrothermal veins or metasomatic deposits associated with silica-rich igneous rocks, generally granites. Associated minerals include topaz, tourmaline, wolframite, quartz and fluorite. Cassiterite is also found in pipe-like bodies with pegmatitic composition which cut limestones and associated with intrusive granite, as in the Kinta Valley, Perak, Malaysia. In Bolivia cassiterite occurs in sulphide veins formed at moderate temperatures. Wood tin found as radially fibrous specimens is formed in the oxidation zone of tin deposits and is found in deposits associated with surface rhyolitic lavas and tuffs.

In England cassiterite is particularly associated with the Cornish mines – Prideaux Wood at Luxulyan and Dolcoath at Camborne, as well as the Turnavore and West Kitty mines at St Agnes (especially noted for wood tin). Other deposits include the Araca mine, Bolivia, which produces facetable material; facetable material is also found at the Erongo tin deposits, Namibia. Tin placers have been economically useful in a number of countries, including Malaysia, Nigeria, Brazil and Bolivia; unfortunately little useful material is found in the United States. Several deposits in Saxony, eastern Germany, have been of some economic importance.

Cassiterite (Brazil)

$$Fe_2O_3$$

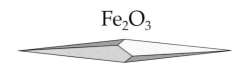

Hematite is the chief ore of iron, although the most important economic deposits do not usually show interesting crystals. It crystallizes in the trigonal system, forming reniform (kidney-shaped) masses or tabular crystals in rosettes. Many other forms occur. The hardness is 5–6 and the specific gravity 5.26. Hematite usually appears black but gives a red streak or powder; thin sections may show steel-grey and the mineral sometimes displays a tarnish of iridescent colours.

Hematite occurs most commonly as thick sedimentary beds. Fine reniform masses are found in Cumbria, England; fine crystals come from the island of Elba, Mount Vesuvius and Mount Etna in Italy, as well as Traversella in Piedmont. Metamorphosed Brazilian sediments provide fine platy crystals, while the Cavradischlucht in Tavetsch, Switzerland, also provides well-formed specimens. Hair-like crystals come from Emmelberg, Eifel in Germany.

LEFT Hematite (St Gotthard, Switzerland)

HALITE

$$NaCl$$

Although salt is very common, it provides beautiful cubic crystals which sometimes take a hollowed-out hopper form. It may also give octahedra or occur in stalactitic masses, the latter characteristic of old mine workings. Halite is a member of the cubic crystal system and shows a perfect cleavage parallel to the cube faces. The hardness is 2.5 and the specific gravity 2.2. It is usually colourless but may show orange, purple or blue tinges. It is soluble in water and some crystals may show a reddish fluorescence from included impurities.

Halite is found in sedimentary deposits, some of which are very large. Good crystals have been found at Wieliczka in Poland, Stassfurt in Germany, Hallstein in Austria, and Lungro in Italy. Halite has been reported from Xinjiang and Qinghai in China.

Halite (Thuringia, Germany)

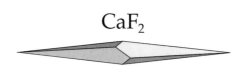

Fluorite appears in almost every mineral collection and the familiar cubic crystals and interpenetrant twins (in green, blue, amber, yellow and pink) make superb centrepieces for display cabinets. A member of the cubic system, fluorite has an octahedral cleavage and a low hardness of 4, so specimens should be handled with care. The specific gravity is 3.18 and the lustre is vitreous, changing to pearly on cleavage surfaces. The term 'fluorescence' derives from fluorite and most specimens show a beautiful blue or violet glow under long-wave ultra-violet radiation. An exception is the mauve-and-white-banded Blue John variety found in Derbyshire, England.

Fluorite is typically found in veins in association with lead and silver ores and also in pneumatolytic deposits with cassiterite, topaz and quartz. Cavities in some sedimentary rocks may contain fluorite with celestine and barite. Alpine clefts provide fine pink to rose-red crystals, and fluorite is a member of the 'Kluftmineralien' eagerly sought in the European Alps. These minerals occur in joints in granite and other igneous rocks.

British deposits occur in the northern Pennine orefield in north-east England, where the Heights mine provided some of the finest green crystal groups ever recorded and the Boltsburn mine some of the finest purple crystals. In Cornwall it is reported from the Trevaunance mine, St Agnes, as well as at Carn Brea, Redruth, Colcerrow and Luxulyan. In Europe rose-coloured crystals have recently been reported from the Zinggenstock in central Switzerland. It is found at the Silius mine in Sardinia and rare crystals of scalenohedral form are found at Wolsendorf, Bavaria, Germany. Purple and golden crystals come from Ehren-friesdorf, Saxony.

Outside Europe fine crystals come from the mining area around Rosiclare, Illinois, USA. Crystals have light yellow bodies with a purple surface. Fine emerald-green crystals occur in veins in the gneiss at Westmoreland, New Hampshire. Fine coloured though small crystals are found in the nepheline syenites at Mont St Hilaire, Quebec, Canada. It has also been noted from Hunan and Anhui, China.

CUMENGEITE

Pb$_{21}$Cu$_{20}$Cl4$_2$(OH)$_{40}$

Cumengeite crystallizes in the tetragonal crystal system, forming cube-like crystals. These are found as overgrowths on boleite and pseudo-boleite crystals. The mineral is indigo-blue with a hardness of 2.5 and specific gravity of 4.6. Crystals are translucent with a sky-blue streak.

Cumengeite is found with boleite and pseudo-boleite at Boleo, Santa Rosalia, Baja California, Mexico. The parallel overgrowths on boleite sometimes envelop the boleite to give the appearance of twinned groups. Cumengeite is less hard than boleite and is soluble in nitric acid.

Fluorite (Graubunden, Switzerland)

Cumengeite [LEFT] and boleite (Baja California, Mexico)

MALACHITE

$$Cu_2(CO_3)(OH)_2$$

Although almost all the malachite seen in ornamental use is the banded massive variety, sprays of crystals of the monoclinic system are found in a number of places. These crystals are virtually always twinned and show a perfect cleavage. The hardness of malachite is 3.5–4.5 and the specific gravity 3.6–4. The green crystals have an adamantine lustre inclining to vitreous and show a pale green streak. They are translucent to opaque. Massive material is concentrically banded and often occurs with azurite. It will effervesce with dilute acids.

Malachite is an ore of copper, but not an important one. It occurs as a secondary mineral in the upper oxidized zone of copper deposits. Some of the finest massive malachite is found at Mednorudyansk and Nizhne-Tagilsk in the USSR. Fine crystals are found at Tsumeb, Namibia, and large quantities of the massive material are found in Zaire.

Malachite (Zimbabwe)

AZURITE

$$Cu_3(CO_3)_2(OH)_2$$

Azurite (Tsumeb, Namibia)

Azurite is often so closely intergrown with the copper carbonate, malachite, that the combined minerals are known as azur-malachite. Azurite, as the name suggests, is a deep azure and crystallizes in the monoclinic crystal system, forming large tabular crystals with a good cleavage, or as rosettes or masses. Crystals have a high lustre sometimes approaching adamantine and their hardness is 3.5–4, with a specific gravity of 3.77. Azurite dissolves with effervescence in hydrochloric acid and thin pieces may be transparent, some having been faceted as gemstones. This material comes from Tsumeb, Namibia.

Azurite has a blue streak and is found as a secondary mineral in the upper oxidized zones of copper deposits. Very fine-coloured masses are characteristic of the deposits at Bisbee, Arizona, USA, where the Copper Queen mine produces the best specimens; fine crystals are also found at Chessy near Lyon, Rhone, France. Other important deposits include Altenmittlau, Spessart in Germany, Rudabanya in Hungary, the Tynagh mine in the Irish Republic, and the Eifel region of Germany. In the Altai fine small crystals are found at Tomsk and Solotuschinsk, and there is a notable Siberian deposit at Beresov. Azurite is found at the celebrated deposit at Broken Hill, New South Wales, Australia.

CALCITE

CaCO$_3$

Dimorphous with aragonite, calcite is the commoner form of calcium carbonate. It is a member of the trigonal system, having perfect cleavage and probably displaying more distinct crystal forms than any other mineral. These include various rhombohedra, scalenohedra and prismatic forms; calcite also forms parallel and subparallel aggregates and masses; several types of twinning are recognized. The hardness is 3 and the specific gravity 2.7.

Calcite is transparent to translucent and faceted clear forms show marked birefringence; large clear crystals are known as Iceland Spar and their clarity makes them ideal for optical use. Calcite is colourless, but it shows a variety of fluorescent effects, the colour of the fluorescence varying according to the activating impurity. Many crystals show phosphorescence and some show triboluminescence (emission of light when rubbed). Calcite will dissolve with effervescence in cold hydrochloric acid.

All types of environment may produce calcite and its occurrence is worldwide. Iceland Spar comes from Helgustedir, Iceland, and fine crystals are found at Egremont in Cumbria, England, and at St Andreasberg in the Harz Mountains of central Germany. Cornish deposits occur at Wheal Wray near Liskeard, and Norwegian finds have been made among the silver deposit at Kongsberg. Some large crystals are found in the USA, especially at the Iceberg claim in the Harding mine at Taos county, New Mexico.

The name alabaster, often incorrectly given to a form of calcite, should be reserved solely for gypsum. Sphaerocobaltite is an allied pink, cobaltian variety.

Calcite (Tennessee, USA)

ARAGONITE

$CaCO_3$

Aragonite (Enna, Sicily)

Aragonite is dimorphous with calcite but crystallizes in the orthorhombic rather than the trigonal system of which calcite is a member. Aragonite crystals are often characteristically twinned, forming pseudo-hexagonal shapes and there is one direction of distinct cleavage. The hardness is 3.5–4 and the specific gravity 2.94. Some Sicilian material may show a green phosphorescence (a glow when the stimulus is removed) after subjection to long-wave ultraviolet radiation. Some large clear crystals, notably those from Horschenz, Germany, which are a straw yellow, have been faceted but the mineral is more commonly collected for its crystals. Aragonite is less common than calcite and is found near the surface as a low-temperature mineral. It may be formed from hot springs and geysers, found as stalactites, in gypsum beds, iron ore deposits, in veins in serpentine, in basalts and in sulphur deposits with celestine. Occurrences of aragonite are worldwide; fine crystals come from Alston Moor, Cleator Moor and Frizington, Cumbria, England, and from the Magdalena district, Socorro county, New Mexico, USA.

DOLOMITE

$$CaMg(CO_3)_2$$

Dolomite is sometimes clear enough to facet and gives colourless to pale yellow gemstones with a marked double refraction. Most material, however, is only translucent. Dolomite is a member of the trigonal crystal system in which it forms masses or rhombohedra with markedly curved faces. There is a perfect rhombohedral cleavage and the hardness is 3.5–4. Dolomite has a specific gravity of 2.85 and faces show a pearly lustre on cleavage surfaces.

Dolomite occurs as rocks, with a worldwide distribution; it may be secondary in origin and may derive from limestones, coral or marble by magnesium-bearing solutions. Many dolomitic rocks are mixtures of calcite and dolomite. Facetable material comes from Egui, Navarra, Spain, and from the Missouri-Oklahoma-Kansas lead deposits, where zinc also occurs. The Lockport dolomite, New York, provides fine crystals, and good quality material also comes from St Eustache, Quebec, Canada.

The famous locality of the Binntal, Switzerland, is rich in dolomite crystals as are the areas of Leogang, Salzburg, Austria, and Traversella, Piedmont, Italy. Dolomite also comes from Rezbanya, Hungary. Dolomite crystals occur at many other places and those listed above are merely a selection.

Dolomite (Spain)

WITHERITE

$BaCO_3$

Witherite (Illinois, USA)

Witherite is an important source of barium and belongs to the orthorhombic crystal system in which it forms twinned crystals appearing as hexagonal dipyramids. It is commonly found as masses. The hardness is 3–3.5 and the specific gravity 4.3. Crystals are colourless to pale yellow, green or brown with a white streak and a green-blue or yellow fluorescence under short-wave ultra-violet radiation, shown especially by material from England. It is soluble in dilute HCl.

Witherite is found with galena and barite in low-temperature hydrothermal veins. There are deposits in the north-east of England, including Fallowfield and Alston Moor, which are still important collecting sites. Fine radiating aggregates come from the Tsubaki silver mine, Japan, and there are large crystals at Rosiclare, Illinois, USA. Austrian deposits occur at Leogang and Peggau. Witherite occurs at several places in the USSR and in France.

SMITHSONITE

$$ZnCO_3$$

Smithsonite (Tsumeb, Namibia)

Smithsonite occurs as white, green or blue-green botryoidal masses or as stalactites of the trigonal crystal system. There is a rhombohedral cleavage, often curved, and the hardness is 4–4.5. The lustre is vitreous, pearly on cleavage faces; the specific gravity is 4.3–4.4. The streak is white and the mineral will effervesce with acids.

Smithsonite is found in the oxidized zone of zinc ore deposits. Specimens are found in the lead and zinc slags at Laurium, Greece, where silver was worked in Roman times; fine green masses occur at the Kelly mine, Socorro County, New Mexico, USA, from Altenberg and Wiesloch in Germany, Bleiberg in Austria, Monteponi and Iglesias in Sardinia, Italy, from Tsumeb, Namibia, where fine, translucent green, jade-like material is found, from Broken Hill, New South Wales, Australia, and from Guangxi, China.

AURICHALCITE

$(Zn,Cu)_5(CO_3)_2(OH)_6$

Blue tufted aggregates of aurichalcite are characteristic of the lead slags found at Laurium, Greece – an area worked for silver since classical times. The mineral is also found at Monteponi in Sardinia, and at Mapimi, Durango in Mexico. It crystallizes in the orthorhombic system and individual crystals have a hardness of 1–2 and a specific gravity of 3.64. Aurichalcite is a secondary mineral found in the oxidized zone of copper deposits. British localities include the Matlock area of Derbyshire and several places in Cumbria. It is found at Leadhills, Lanarkshire, Scotland.

Aurichalcite (Arizona, USA)

CERUSSITE

PbCO$_3$

Crystals of cerussite occur in many forms within the orthorhombic system. The most interesting are the star-like pseudo-hexagonal twins, the finest of which are found at Tsumeb, Namibia. Cerussite, with a hardness of 3–3.5, has a distinct cleavage and is brittle. This makes it hard to facet, even though cut stones show a high dispersion. The specific gravity is 6.5 and the lustre adamantine. Many crystals are transparent, but some are translucent. Under short-wave ultra-violet radiation some cerussite glows pale green or blue. The streak is white or colourless.

Cerussite is found in the upper oxidized zones of lead ore deposits, where it occurs with other lead, zinc or copper minerals; these include anglesite, pyromorphite, phosgenite and smithsonite.

Fine specimens come from the Sardinian lead deposits at Monteponi and at Montevecchio. Smaller but well-formed crystals are found in the Scottish lead-mining district at Leadhills, Lanarkshire, where it is found with leadhillite and caledonite. It is found in the USSR in the Nerchinsk district of Transbaikalia and at Beresov in the Urals. Twinned reticular (net-like) aggregates are found at Broken Hill, New South Wales, Australia. Although Cornwall is not primarily known as a lead-mining area, crystals of cerussite were once found at the Pentire Glaze mine, St Minver.

Cerussite (Tsumeb, Namibia)

RHODOCHROSITE

$MnCO_3$

Rose-red masses of opaque rhodochrosite were once the only known specimens but in recent years more and more transparent single crystals have come on to the market, some of magnificent orange-pink colour. These form scalenohedral crystal groups of the trigonal system with a perfect rhombohedral cleavage and a hardness of 3.5–4. The specific gravity is 3.7 and the lustre vitreous inclining to pearly. It has a white streak and is soluble with effervescence in warm acids.

Rhodochrosite single crystals and scalenohedral groups at their finest come from the Kalahari region of South Africa, particularly from the Hotazel and N'Chwaning mines. The mineral is characteristic of moderate- to low-temperature hydrothermal vein deposits with silver, lead, zinc and copper ores; it also occurs in high-temperature metamorphic deposits with garnet and rhodonite. It is also characteristic of manganese deposits of secondary origin.

Rhodochrosite of good quality is found in Germany at the Wolf mine, Herdorf, Siegerland, at Rheinbreitbach and Freiburg, at Trepca in Yugoslavia, Madem Laccos in northern Greece, Les Cabesses in the Pyrenees, France, and from the province of Huelva, Spain. Rhodochrosite is found at the Huallapon mine, Pasto Bueno, Peru, and in the provinces of Catamarca and La Rioja, Argentina. In the USA it is found in Colorado around Leadville and in the Home Sweet Home mine, Alma. Deposits have also been found at the Oppu mine, Japan.

Some transparent material has come from Magdalena, Mexico, and several places in Romania have produced collectable specimens. It is known from the state of Minas Gerais, Brazil, and from the northern Urals and Siberia, USSR. Rhodochrosite may be faceted despite the cleavage, though the best crystals are so beautiful that they are never likely to be cut.

Rhodochrosite (Nassau, Germany)

SIDERITE

FeCO$_3$

Although siderite is a fairly common and well-distributed mineral, relatively few specimens are sought by collectors, but some may be faceted as very rare gemstones. Siderite is a member of the trigonal crystal system in which it forms rhombohedral or scalenohedral crystals. The hardness is 3.5–4.5 and there is a perfect rhombohedral cleavage. The colour ranges from yellowish-brown to green or brown and the specific gravity is 3.9. The lustre may be vitreous to pearly or silky and some surfaces may show an iridescent tarnish. Siderite is slowly soluble in cold acids and more rapidly in hot. Crystals are transparent to translucent.

Economically important deposits of siderite occur in bedded sediments with shale or coal seams. It occurs in hydrothermal metallic veins and in basaltic rocks. It is found in some pegmatites and occurs as a replacement of limestones by iron solutions. Fine crystals occur at Traversella, Piedmont, Italy, and at Tavetsch, Grisons, Switzerland. In England well-crystallized material is found in Cornwall at the Great Onslow Consols mine, St Breward, at Wheal Maudlin, Lanlivery, and the Penlee quarry, St Just. In Devon siderite occurs at the Virtuous Lady mine, Buckland Monachorum. It is found at Panasqueira, Portugal, and occurs in pegmatite-pneumatolytic areas of Ivigtut, Greenland. Good crystals come from the silver-lead mines of Idaho, USA, particularly at Coeur d'Alene.

Siderite (Cornwall, England)

DIOPTASE

$$CuSiO_2(OH)_2$$

Dioptase (Reneville, Zaire)

Fine dark green crystal groups of dioptase can be found in almost all mineral collections. A deeper, more intense green than that of emerald, dioptase has a hardness of 5 and a perfect rhombohedral cleavage which betrays its membership of the trigonal crystal system. The specific gravity is 3.28–3.35; stones are rarely faceted because of the cleavage, and the green is too deep to show the high dispersion possessed by the mineral.

Dioptase, which is transparent to translucent, is found in the oxidized zone of copper deposits. Most of the spectacular groups in museums come from the Tsumeb area of Namibia, especially from the Omaue mine, Kaoko-Veld. These groups are closely rivalled by those from Katanga, Zaire. It is found in the Altyn-Tube area of the Khirgiz steppes, USSR, and among the copper deposits at Copiapo, Chile.

CHRYSOCOLLA

$$(Cu,Al)_2H_2Si_2O_5(OH)_4 \cdot nH_2O$$

Although crystallizing in the monoclinic system, chrysocolla is found as aggregates which have a hardness of just over 2; however, if the chrysocolla is heavily impregnated with quartz, it increases to 7. The specific gravity is approximately 2.6 and the lustre is dull, becoming vitreous when quartz is present. Like most copper minerals, the colour is blue to green. The mineral is sectile and specimens may adhere to the tongue; it may be mixed with copper carbonates or with turquoise.

Chrysocolla is found in the oxidized zones of copper deposits. A variety in which it is mixed with malachite is known as Eilat stone, referring to the place on the Gulf of Aqaba where it is found. Silica-poor specimens are easily broken.

Fine specimens in which quartz is impregnated by chrysocolla come from the Globe mine, Gila County, Arizona, USA. English deposits occur in Cornwall and Cumbria, but high-quality specimens are rare occurrences today. Chrysocolla is also found at Johnsbach, Steiermark, Austria, and in the Katanga area of Zaire.

Chrysocolla (Arizona, USA)

PHENAKITE

$$Be_2SiO_4$$

Phenakite is a member of the trigonal crystal system in which it forms rhombohedral crystals which are often twinned. The hardness is 7.5–8 and the specific gravity 2.93–3.00. Phenakite is most commonly colourless but may be tinged with yellow or pink. The lustre is vitreous; most material is transparent to translucent. Phenakite is found in granite pegmatites, hydrothermal veins and Alpine-type deposits. Most specimens in collections and the fairly rare faceted stones come from locations in the state of Minas Gerais, Brazil, particularly San Miguel di Piracicaba. It is also found beside the Takowaya River in the Ural Mountains, USSR. Fine bluish crystals come from Lago Bianco, Ticino in Switzerland, from Bockstein, Austria, and Drammen, Norway. Good specimens have been found in pegmatite pockets with beryl at Mount Antero, Colorado, USA.

RIGHT Phenakite on beryl (Colorado, USA)

WOLLASTONITE

CaSiO$_3$

Wollastonite forms tabular crystals, often twinned, or fibrous masses of the triclinic crystal system. There is a perfect cleavage and the hardness is 4.5–5. The colour is grey, white or very pale green, and some specimens show fluorescence, usually yellow or orange under long-wave ultra-violet radiation. The specific gravity is 2.87–3.09 and the lustre is vitreous or pearly. Most wollastonite is translucent.

The mineral is found in metamorphosed limestones and much specimen material comes from the mines of the New Jersey Zinc Company at Franklin, USA. Fibrous masses are found at Perheniemi, Finland.

Wollastonite (New York, USA)

PECTOLITE

$$NaCa_2Si_3O_8OH$$

Pectolite (New Jersey, USA)

Collectors may know pectolite best from the pale blue to medium blue translucent ornamental variety to which the name Larimar has been given. More commonly pectolite occurs as mamillary masses of needle-like crystals of the triclinic system. There is a perfect cleavage but the mineral also tends to crumble into fibres. The hardness is 4.5–5 and the specific gravity 2.74–2.88. It is colourless to pale blue and translucent with a vitreous to silky lustre. Some specimens may show an orange fluorescence under long-wave ultra-violet radiation. Pectolite is found in cavities in basaltic rock with zeolite minerals. Larimar comes from the Dominican Republic; other varieties come from the trap rocks in New Jersey, USA. As tiny crystals may penetrate the skin, pectolite should not be handled. Fine crystals are found at a number of Canadian locations.

DIOPSIDE

$$CaMgSi_2O_6$$

Diopside (Quebec, Canada)

Diopside is an important member of the pyroxene mineral group, membership which it shares with jadeite and spodumene. It forms stubby crystals in the monoclinic system, with a perfect cleavage and a hardness of 5.5–6.5. The specific gravity is 3.22–3.38. The colour ranges from a light green, sometimes an emerald green where chromium is present, to brown. Some diopside, when appropriately cut, may show a four-rayed star, and some light-coloured crystals from dolomitic marble may show a blue fluorescence.

Diopside is found in calcium-rich metamorphic rocks; some green crystals are found in kimber-lites, the serpentinized olivine rock which may contain diamond, and they may occur as recognizable green inclusions in diamond. Fine chrome-green specimens are found at Outukumpu, Finland, and in the Ural Mountains of the USSR. Diopside also occurs in Burma where violet and yellow varieties are found in the northern gem-bearing areas.

Good crystals come from the Zillertal, Austria, and fine green crystals are found in Italy at Val d'Ossola, Novara. Green crystals from De Kalb, New York, USA, can be found in many mineral collections.

SPHENE

$$CaTiSiO_5$$

Sphene (Capelinha, Brazil)

Sometimes known as titanite, sphene forms wedge-shaped crystals in the monoclinic system. The crystals are often twinned and much sphene occurs as masses. The cleavage is distinct and the hardness 5–5.5. Colours include green and a rare emerald-green where chromium is present, yellow and brown to black. The specific gravity is 3.45–3.55 and the lustre is adamantine to resinous. The streak is white; faceted sphene shows a high dispersion.

This mineral is found in igneous and metamorphic rocks and is common in nepheline syenites. Fine crystals occur in Alpine locations, including Pfitsch, Tirol in Austria, the St Gotthard Pass and Tavetsch in Switzerland. Other locations in this part of Europe include Teufelsmühle, Habachtal and Bruchgraben, Hollersbachtal in Austria. Tabular crystals form veins in silicate rock at Kragerö, Norway. Good gem-quality material comes from a pegmatite at Capelinha, Minas Gerais, Brazil. Yellow-brown transparent crystals were once found at the Tilly Foster mine, Brewster, New York, USA. Yellow gem-quality crystals come from the Gardiner complex in Greenland, and emerald green chrome sphene comes from a location in Baja California, Mexico.

ZIRCON

ZrSiO$_4$

A well-known gem mineral which, when cut in its colourless form, is an acceptable substitute for diamond. Zircon has an interesting chemical history. In fact, zircon is said to be 'high' or 'low' according to the degree of breakdown suffered by its crystal structure over geological time. The breakdown is caused by radioactive particles included in the crystals which have a long-term effect on the stability of the mineral; the older the rock in which a zircon was formed, the less crystalline it becomes, since the cumulative effect of the particle bombardment is to make the crystal virtually amorphous, or non-crystalline. In practice these low zircons (known as 'metamict') occur in Sri Lanka, and the high zircons, in which the process has scarcely begun, come from Indo-China and other areas.

Zircons comprise a wide range of quiet colours and many need to be heated to give the blue, golden and colourless faceted stones which are traditionally popular in jewellery. Colourless stones show a high dispersion – the breaking up of white light into its spectrum colours – and rival diamond in this respect; they are softer, however, and are also doubly refractive, which means that back facet edges appear doubled when observed through the top of the faceted stone. This effect is impossible in diamond.

Zircons are minerals of igneous rocks but are virtually always found in alluvial deposits. Metamict stones are usually green or brown, though not all green or brown stones are metamict; other crystals are usually brownish when found and gain their colour by heating. Constants vary with the degree of metamictization: the hardness is usually near 7 and the specific gravity 4.6 decreasing to 4.0. The refractive index may reach 2.01 at its highest. Crystals of the tetragonal system are hard to find, zircon being found mostly as water-worn pebbles, but bipyramids are possible, as are prismatic crystals terminated by pyramid forms.

Zircon (South Carolina, USA)

SERANDITE

$Na(Mn^{2+},Ca)_2Si_3O_8(OH)$

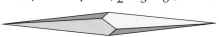

Serandite (Quebec, Canada)

Stubby crystals of serandite belong to the triclinic crystal system and have a perfect cleavage. The hardness is 4.5–5 and the specific gravity 3.32. Serandite is rose red to salmon red with a vitreous to pearly lustre. Serandite is found in nepheline syenite rocks at Mont Saint Hilaire, Quebec, Canada. It has also been found on the Los Islands of Guinea. It is very rarely fashioned as a gemstone but, when cut, shows a magnificent orange-pink.

OLIVINE

$(Mg,Fe)_2SiO_4$

Olivine (Egypt)

Olivine is used to name both an important mineral and a rock largely composed of that mineral. To the gemmologist olivine means the gemstone peridot – the oily, olive-green stone which is sometimes found in very large sizes. Olivine is always dark as it belongs to the group of dark ferromagnesian minerals, and some crystals are brown. It is found in igneous rocks, major sources occurring on the Island of St John in the Red Sea, in Burma, Hawaii and the south-western states of the USA. It is fairly hard, about 6.5–7, but has two directions of cleavage, meaning that stones have to be handled carefully; the specific gravity is 3.34

and the refractive index 1.65–1.69. The green and brown colours come from the iron which is an essential part of the mineral's composition.

Olivine is a member of the orthorhombic crystal system but well-developed crystals are rare as the low hardness cannot resist abrasion very well. Chemically the magnesium and iron silicates of the olivine family are minerals in themselves and there is a complete series between the two; the magnesium silicate is forsterite and the iron silicate fayalite. Peridot comes somewhere between the two extremes, so the composition as written above could indicate a peridot specimen.

KYANITE

Al$_2$SiO$_5$

Kyanite has the same chemical composition as the important minerals andalusite and sillimanite, although the three vary structurally. Kyanite is well known to mineralogists for its marked directional hardness (7.5 across the crystal, 4.5 along the length) and for its attractive blue to green colour. Many crystals show a blue stripe against a light green background and, despite the perfect cleavage, have been cut as gemstones.

Kyanite forms flattened bladed crystals of the triclinic system; the lustre is vitreous, changing to pearly on cleavage surfaces. The specific gravity is 3.68. It shows strong pleochroism – a change in colour with direction.

Kyanite is a characteristic mineral of metamorphic rocks, especially schists and gneisses. It may also be found in granite pegmatites. It is typical of the Alpine regions, locations including Pizzo Forno, Ticino in Switzerland, and Hohe Tauern and other regions of Austria. Large, transparent crystals come from Kenya and the state of Minas Gerais in Brazil. It has recently been reported from the Xinjiang Autonomous Region in China.

Kyanite (North Carolina, USA)

SPODUMENE

LiAlSi$_2$O$_6$

A member of the important pyroxene mineral group, spodumene crystallizes in the monoclinic system, forming characteristic flattened prismatic crystals with vertical striations and a perfect prismatic cleavage. The hardness is 6.5–7.5 and the specific gravity 3.0–3.2. Spodumene may be colourless, yellow, pink, green, emerald-green or violet. The lustre is vitreous; some crystals fluoresce under long-wave ultra-violet radiation, the colour being most commonly orange with a phosphorescence of the same colour. Spodumene is transparent to translucent.

The mineral is characteristic of granite pegmatites. Some varieties provide gem material, notably the lilac kunzite, green iron-bearing material and emerald-green chrome-bearing material only from North Carolina, USA. Yellow crystals come from Afghanistan and Pakistan, while fine kunzite comes from Pala, southern California, USA, and from Madagascar. Spodumene has been reported from Xingjiang, China. However, the main source of gem-quality spodumene is the state of Minas Gerais, Brazil, where the green, yellow and kunzite varieties are found.

Spodumene (California, USA)

NATROLITE

$$Na_2Ca_2Si_3O_{10}.2H_2O$$

White natrolite forms slender, needle-like crystals with a square cross-section and terminated by a four-faced pyramid. Alternatively, it forms fibrous masses. It is a member of the orthorhombic crystal system and has a perfect cleavage, with a hardness of 5.5 and a specific gravity of 2.2–2.3. The lustre is pearly and silky in the fibrous specimens. Some examples may show an orange fluorescence under long-wave ultra-violet radiation. Natrolite is transparent to translucent.

A member of the zeolite group of minerals, natrolite occurs in basaltic cavities and in other dark igneous rocks. Material from Bound Brook, New Jersey, USA, may be found sufficiently transparent to be faceted. Other occurrences include the Fassa valley, south Tirol in Austria, Teplice and Aussig in Czechoslovakia, Alpstein, Hesse in Germany, and Antronapiana, Ossola, Novara in Italy. It is also found in the Kola Peninsula, USSR, Phillip Island, Victoria, Australia, Mont Saint Hilaire, Quebec, Canada, where it is found in pegmatites, and at Kimberley, South Africa. It has been found together with scolecite at Poona, India.

Natrolite. (New Jersey, USA)

LEUCITE

KAlSi$_2$O$_6$

Leucite (Rocca Monfina, Italy)

Virtually all fine leucite crystals, some transparent enough to facet, come from the Alban Hills near Rome, Italy. They display pseudocubic form in the tetragonal crystal system and appear as icositetrahedra. The hardness is 5.5–6 and crystals are white to colourless. Leucite has a specific gravity of 2.47–2.5, is translucent to opaque and has a colourless streak. Cut stones may show interference colours and some Italian material may give a medium to bright orange fluorescence in long-wave ultra-violet radiation, and under X-rays it may glow blue.

Apart from the Alban Hills deposits, much leucite comes from Vesuvius and Mount Somma, where it occurs as ejected masses or as perfect crystals in lava. It also occurs at the Laacher See, Eifel in Germany, and at Magnet Cove, Arkansas, USA.

MICROCLINE

KAlSi$_3$O$_8$

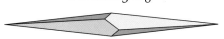

Microcline is a member of the potassium group of the feldspar family but unlike the other members of the group it belongs to the triclinic crystal system. The name reflects the way in which the crystal symmetry only just falls into this system, in which the crystallographic axes are all inclined to one another. The crystals are a characteristic green with white streaks and are usually twinned to form attractive groups. The hardness is 6–6.5 and the specific gravity 2.54–2.63. Microcline is almost always opaque and is found in pegmatites, schists, granites and syenites, as well as in acidic plutonic rock. Fine crystal groups come from Amelia, Virginia and Pike's Peak, Colorado, USA.

Microcline (Colorado, USA)

Orthoclase (Nevada, USA)

A member of the feldspar mineral group orthoclase gives the gem moonstone and also forms beautiful transparent yellow crystals which are sometimes faceted. The feldspars are either potassium aluminium silicates or sodium-calcium aluminium silicates; orthoclase is a member of the first group and the moonstone effect is created when thin plates of albite, the sodium feldspar, are included in orthoclase. Light reflected from the included crystals gives the characteristic glow. Orthoclase is a member of the monoclinic crystal system and is the standard 6 on Mohs' scale of hardness. There is a perfect cleavage and the specific gravity is 2.5–2.6. The lustre is vitreous.

Orthoclase is a mineral of pegmatites and the finest yellow crystals are found in the Itrongay pegmatites of Madagascar. The best orthoclase moonstone (other feldspar members may show the moonstone effect) comes from Alpine regions, Burma and Sri Lanka. The specific gravity of orthoclase moonstone is 2.56–2.59.

ALBITE

NaAlSi$_3$O$_8$

Albite is a member of the plagioclase group of the feldspar family of minerals. It forms twinned platy crystals in white, yellow, pink, green, grey, reddish and colourless varieties though all the colours are subdued. It is a member of the triclinic crystal system, has a hardness of 6–6.5 and specific gravity of 2.63. It forms inclusions in orthoclase to give moonstone but albite is also capable of giving a moonstone effect on its own. Some albite from Madagascar is transparent enough to facet. Albite forms at low temperatures and is found in pegmatites, marbles and granites.

Albite (Graubunden, Switzerland)

BERYL

$$Be_3Al_2(SiO_3)_6$$

This important mineral family includes the gem species emerald and aquamarine as well as pink and yellow beryl which also have ornamental application. Most beryl varieties are found in the igneous rocks known as pegmatites, though emerald is more commonly found in shales or talc-carbonate schists. The colour of emerald is derived from a somewhat small amount of chromium impurity; yellow and blue beryls are coloured by iron.

As an important gemstone, emerald is frequently imitated and it can also be made in the laboratory. Examination of the interior of the stone

Beryl (Utah, USA)

Beryl (Colombia)

with a microscope is the best way of distinguishing the genuine article from the imitation, and emeralds from different mines can also be distinguished by their inclusions – fragments of other minerals or tiny liquid or gas patterns which are characteristic of different locations. The finest quality emeralds come from Colombia; stones from Pakistan are also of superb colour, but so far they have been found only in fairly small sizes. The Sandawana emeralds from Zimbabwe are also of magnificent colour and retain their brilliance even in small stones.

Brazilian emeralds are more heavily included; those from Siberia are bright and clear, though rarely seen on the market. The finest aquamarines come from Brazil and ideally should be a deep blue in one direction and a lighter blue at right angles to this direction. Stones of a watery or pale blue shade are less valuable. The best yellow

Beryl (Pakistan)

Beryl (Ukraine, USSR)

beryls should be distinctly golden, very similar to the sun; in fact, the name heliodor has been used for them (derived from *helios*, the Greek word for sun). Pink beryl is called morganite and very fine specimens come from Madagascar and California. The stone is characteristically peach-coloured rather than the reddish-pink suggested by its name.

A number of years ago red beryls coloured by manganese were discovered in deposits of rhyolite, a fine-grained igneous rock, at two places in Utah, United States. At their very best the stones are a fine, dark red, though most have a tinge of brown. Beryl has a hardness of 7.5, a specific gravity of 2.69–2.71 and refractive indices in the range 1.57–1.59. It is a member of the hexagonal crystal system, forming prismatic crystals with a hexagonal cross-section.

EUCLASE

BeAlSiO$_4$(OH)

Named for its easy cleavage, euclase is a member of the monoclinic crystal system in which it forms tabular or prismatic crystals with a hardness of 6.5–7.5 and a specific gravity of 3. The colours range from yellow through pale green to blue; colourless material is also known. Some sapphire blue crystals have been found in Zimbabwe.

Euclase is a characteristic mineral of granite pegmatites and some transparent pieces have been faceted, though the cleavage makes this process difficult. Most gem material comes from the state of Minas Gerais, Brazil. It is also found from the Sanarka river, USSR, and dark blue crystals have been reported from the emerald deposits of Colombia. Finds have also been made in the Windtal, South Tirol, Austria.

Euclase (Zimbabwe)

GROSSULAR

$Ca_3Al_2(SiO_4)_3$

Grossular is a member of the garnet group of minerals and like other members crystallizes in the cubic crystal system. Though many think of garnet as red, this colour is not found in grossular although it does provide a very attractive range of other colours. It forms rhombic dodecahedra, icositetrahedra or combinations of the two forms; some varieties are found only as shapeless lumps. Grossular has a hardness of 6.5–7 and a specific gravity of 3.4–3.6. Specimens may be colourless, orange, yellow, green or brown. The lustre is vitreous and the streak white. Grossular is found in metamorphosed impure calcareous rocks, especially in contact zones. The variety tsavolite is emerald-green from a small chromium impurity and is found in Kenya and Pakistan. The cinnamon-brown hessonite is found in a number of places, particularly in Sri Lanka, Brazil and many other places. Particularly attractive crystal groups of orange hessonite come from Eden Mills, Vermont, USA. Hydrogrossular, a translucent dark green, comes from South Africa and may be mistaken for one of the jade minerals. Grossular shows so great a variety of colours because it forms chemical links with other members of the garnet group and thus borrows some of their characteristics. Much grossular is transparent so it has considerable gemstone potential.

Grossular (Vermont, USA)

PREHNITE

$$Ca_2Al_2Si_2O_{10}(OH)_2$$

Prehnite usually occurs as compact botryoidal masses or as tabular crystals of the orthorhombic system with a distinct basal cleavage. The hardness is 6–6.5 and the specific gravity 2.90–2.95. Prehnite is pale to dark green, yellow or grey to colourless. The lustre is vitreous to pearly and the streak colourless. Prehnite is translucent to near-transparent. It is found as a second stage mineral in cavities in basic igneous rocks; it also occurs in gneiss, granite and metamorphosed limestones. Fine crystals come from European Alpine locations, including the Fassa Valley and Seiser Alm, Tirol in Austria, Haslach, Schwarzwald in Germany, Bourg d'Oisans, Dauphiné in France, and Montecatini, Italy. It is found at the Jeffrey mine, Asbestos, Quebec, Canada, in the trap rocks of New Jersey in the Paterson area, and at Crestmore, California, USA.

Prehnite (New Jersey, USA)

LABRADORITE

$$NaAlSi_3O_8 - CaAl_2Si_2O_8$$

Labradorite is a member of the sodium-aluminium series of the feldspar group of minerals (the plagioclase feldspars) and is celebrated for its opal-like play of colours against a dark background, although transparent labradorite in a variety of rather pale colours is known. Some labradorite contains profuse hematite inclusions which give an overall reddish or golden sheen. The play of colour is caused by included lamellae of other feldspar minerals and is known as schiller or labradorescence.

Labradorite has a hardness of 6–6.5 and a specific gravity of 2.69–2.72. It is found in dark igneous rocks and fine material comes from Norway and Finland. Transparent labradorite is found in Utah and California, USA. Some labradorite may give a moonstone effect; this can be seen in some Madagascan material.

Labradorite (Labrador, Canada)

STILBITE

$$NaCa_2Al_5Si_{13}O_{36}.14H_2O$$

Stilbite (New South Wales, Australia)

Stilbite, which forms crystals in the monoclinic and triclinic systems, is a member of the zeolite group of minerals in which it appears as cruciform penetration twins or as masses. There is a perfect cleavage and the hardness is 3.5–4. Stilbite is white, grey, yellowish, orange, pink or light brown with a vitreous lustre, pearly on cleavage surfaces. The specific gravity is 2.09–2.2 and the streak is colourless.

Stilbite is found in cavities in basalt, andesite and related volcanic rocks, also from cavities in pegmatites and in some hot spring deposits. It occurs in the trap rocks of New Jersey and in Cowlitz county, Washington, USA. Bright orange crystals come from Kilpatrick, Scotland, and from Great Notch, New Jersey, USA. It is also to be found in Brazil and in India, in the famous Deccan trap rocks.

SPESSARTINE

$$Mn_3Al_2(SiO_4)_3$$

Spessartine (California, USA)

A member of the garnet family, spessartine forms rhombic dodecahedra or icositetrahedra of the cubic crystal system, or combinations of the two forms. The hardness is 7–7.5. and the specific gravity 3.8–4.2. Spessartine forms a series with almandine and when rich in iron is a dark red; when there is little iron the manganese gives a pale orange which deepens with increasing iron content. The lustre is vitreous.

Spessartine is found in granite pegmatites, gneisses and schists. Very fine crystals come from the Rutherford pegmatite in Amelia, Virginia, from the Ramona mine, San Diego county, California, and from a rhyolite deposit near Ely, White Pine county, Nevada, USA. Much gem quality material comes from Brazil. It also occurs with galena at Broken Hill, New South Wales, Australia.

ALMANDINE

$$Fe_3Al_2(SiO_4)_3$$

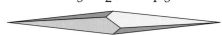

Most of the red garnet so familiar in Victorian and other jewellery is almandine. The colour varies from a bright red where chromium is present to a dark blood-red which appears black unless light can be induced to pass through it by careful cutting. Red garnets form part of a complete chemical series between magnesium aluminium silicate (mineral pyrope) and almandine at the iron end of the series. Almandine crystallizes in the cubic system, forming rhombic dodecahedra, icositetrahedra and combinations of the two. The hardness is 7–7.5 and the specific gravity 3.9–4.3. Almandine occurs in metamorphic rocks as well as in igneous rocks and in contact zones. Much gem-quality material comes from Sri Lanka; fine crystals are found in many other places, especially the Wrangell deposit on the Strikine river estuary, Alaska.

Almandine (Connecticut, USA)

STAUROLITE

$(Fe,Mg,Zn)_2Al_9(SiAl)_4O_{22}(OH)_2$

ABOVE AND RIGHT Staurolite (Georgia, USA)

Staurolite's cross-like twinned crystals are well known to collectors. The mineral crystallizes in the monoclinic system, forming pseudo-orthorhombic crystals with a distinct cleavage and a hardness of 7–7.5. The colour when transparent is a dark to yellowish-green and the lustre is vitreous to resinous. The specific gravity is 3.65–3.83 and the streak is grey.

Staurolite is translucent to transparent and is found in metamorphic rocks, including schists and gneisses. Cross-like crystals are found in the USA states of Virginia, North Carolina and Georgia, and fine crystals are found at Monte Campione, Switzerland, where deposits occur with kyanite. Staurolite also comes from the Hohe Tauern, Austria, and the Gorob mine, Namibia.

EPIDOTE

$$Ca_2(Al,Fe^{3+})_3(SiO_4)_3(OH)$$

Epidote crystallizes in the monoclinic system and forms prismatic or tabular crystals, frequently twinned. Much epidote is found as masses. Crystals show a perfect cleavage and have a hardness of 6–7. The specific gravity is 3.38–3.49. The lustre is vitreous and transparent crystals are often a characteristic pistachio-green ranging to brown. There is a strong pleochroism, so crystals show a change of colour with direction.

Epidote is found in low- to medium-grade metamorphic rocks. Fine crystals come from the Green Monster deposit, Prince of Wales Island, Alaska, USA, and there are many European deposits giving attractive crystals, particularly from Alpine locations. Swiss deposits occur at Gotthard and Tavetsch; Austrian ones in the Hohe Tauern and Untersulzbachtal, Knappenwand being particularly important in the latter area. The state of Minas Gerais, Brazil, produces epidote, and the Baveno area near Lake Maggiore, Italy, is also a good location. Fine yellow and pink-mixed crystals of epidote, clinozoisite and piemontite come from Poncione Alzasca, Ticino, Switzerland. Epidote has been reported from Hebei, China. Fine crystals have also been reported from the Julie claim, Mineral county, Nevada, USA.

Epidote (Pakistan)

VESUVIANITE

$$Ca_{10}Mg_2Al_4(SiO_4)_5(Si_2O_7)_2(OH)_4$$

Sometimes named idocrase, vesuvianite forms well-shaped prismatic crystals of the tetragonal system; the variety californite occurs as masses and is a mixture of vesuvianite and grossular garnet. The hardness of vesuvianite is 6–7 and the specific gravity 3.32–3.47 (that of californite is 3.25–3.32). The colour is yellow or reddish to shades of green to brown. The lustre is vitreous and the mineral transparent to translucent.

Vesuvianite is found in serpentinites and in contact metamorphic deposits. Fine chrome green material has been found at the Jeffrey mine, Asbestos, Quebec, Canada, and in the neighbour-hood of Quetta, Pakistan. Clear brown crystals have been found in Kenya and vesuvianite is also recorded from Pfitsch, Tirol in Austria, Zermatt in Switzerland, Canzocoli and Predazzo, Fassa valley and Monte Somma in Italy, Italian Mountain, Colorado, and large brown crystals from Amity, New York, United States.

Fine massive blue material is to be found in Telemark, Norway. Specimens of a sufficiently clear colouration have occasionally been faceted as gemstones and californite has occassionally been mistaken for, and no doubt has sometimes been offered as, jade.

Vesuvianite (Quebec, Canada)

APOPHYLLITE

$KCa_4Si_8O_{20}(F,OH).8H_2O$

There are two varieties of apophyllite (fluor-apophyllite and hydroxylapophyllite). The best known crystals of all are those from the igneous rocks in the Bombay area of India. Here apophyllite crystals occur as secondary minerals. Many of these tend to be green to a silvery-white colour; they are sometimes faceted, although the perfect cleavage leaves many fine crystals in their original state. Apophyllite is a member of the tetragonal crystal system in which it forms cube-like crystals with a hardness of 4.5–5. The specific gravity is 2.3–2.5.

Apophyllite (New Jersey, USA)

TOPAZ

$$Al_2(F,OH)_2SiO_4$$

Years ago all yellow gemstones were indiscriminately called topaz. Many were actually the citrine variety of quartz and the name topaz was held to improve sales. Topaz is a hard mineral forming crystals of the orthorhombic system with characteristic pyramid and dome terminations with a flat bottom denoting the easy cleavage which takes place in that direction. The colour ranges from yellow through golden to a deep orange-red; crystals from Katlang, Pakistan, are a beautiful deep pink. Topaz is a mineral of pegmatites as the generally large size of many crystals suggests. Most crystals used for gemstones come from the state of Minas Gerais in Brazil, although attractive crystals can be found in many other places; those from the tin-mining areas of Nigeria, for example, display many crystal faces but they lack colour.

Today many blue topazes are on the market. The colour is enhanced in some specimens by a combination of heating and irradiation but natural blue topaz, albeit of a slightly less electric blue, does exist at a number of locations, including the St Anne mine in Zimbabwe. Topaz has a hardness of 8, specific gravity of 3.53 and refractive index 1.62–1.64. The easy cleavage means that cut stones should be handled with care and not dropped on to hard surfaces.

Topaz (Utah, USA)

ELBAITE

$$Na(Li,Al)_3Al_6(BO_3)_3Si_6O_{18}(OH)_4$$

Elbaite (Minas Gerais, Brazil)

Elbaite is one of the members of the tourmaline group of minerals and provides many of the finest gem specimens. It is a member of the trigonal crystal system and occurs as long, prismatic, striated crystals which show pyroelectricity, i.e. they develop an electric charge on heating and thus attract dust. The hardness is 7.25 and the specific gravity 3.03–3.10. The constants vary, like those of all members of the tourmaline group in which there is extensive chemical substitution. The lustre is vitreous and the colours range from red through yellow, green and blue. Many crystals show more than one colour, either as a core or along the length. The streak is colourless.

The tourmaline minerals are characteristic of pegmatites and many places in the Brazilian state of Minas Gerais produce good crystals. Fine pinks are characteristic of the US pegmatites of Pala, San Diego county, California, and Maine, where the Mount Mica tourmaline crystals were some of the first to be discovered in North America. Elbaite is also found in the USSR, Namibia, Sri Lanka, Madagascar, and Laghman, Afghanistan. Bright grass-green, yellow to amber, manganese-rich crystals are found in pegmatites at Sankhuwa Sabha district, Kosi zone, eastern Nepal.

Recently elbaite has been reported from places in China, including Xinjiang Uygur Autonomous Region. A bright blue tourmaline containing copper is found in the state of Paraiba, Brazil.

LAPIS LAZULI

The ornamental blue lapis lazuli is a rock composed of the minerals lazurite, hauyne, sodalite and nosean, which are members of the sodalite group. It is not always easy to determine which minerals are major constituents of a particular specimen, but lapis has a hardness of 5–6 and a specific gravity of 2.7–2.9; if the rock contains pyrite the figure will rise further. Calcite is also frequently included but its whitish patches detract from the value.

Both lapis lazuli and lazurite are found as contact metamorphic minerals in limestones and granites. The best material – blue with no hint of white – comes from Badakshan, Afghanistan; much of the lapis containing prominent calcite comes from the Chilean Andes. Good material from northern Pakistan. This material may show patchy orange fluorescence from the calcite.

Lapis Lazuli (Ovalle, Chile)

TURQUOISE

$$CuAl_6(PO_4)_4(OH)_8.4-5H_2O$$

Turquoise (Virginia, USA)

Turquoise crystals are rare, most material occurring in stalactites or as masses. It is a member of the triclinic system, the rare crystals being short prismatic. The hardness is 5–6 and the specific gravity 2.6–2.8. The colour is pale to sky-blue to bluish-green with a waxy lustre.

Turquoise is found as a secondary mineral formed by the action of surface waters on aluminous rocks. The best gem-quality material comes from Nishapur, Iran, particularly from the Abdurrezzagi mine, Maden. The south-western states of the USA produce a good deal of turquoise but the quality is less fine. Small crystals are known from Lynch, Virginia, and finds have been made in Los Cerillos mountains, New Mexico. Fine dark blue turquoise is reported from Bisbee, Arizona, and from Leadville, Colorado. Turquoise is reported from Chile and Australia. In England it has been found in Cornwall, particularly from the West Phoenix mine, Linkinhorne.

WAVELLITE

$$Al_3(PO_4)_2(OH,F)_3.5H_2O$$

Wavellite (Arkansas, USA)

Collectors value the acicular radiating aggregates of wavellite crystals which belong to the orthorhombic crystal system. There is a perfect cleavage and the hardness is 3.25–4. Wavellite is white, greenish-white or yellow to yellowish-brown, with a vitreous or pearly lustre and a white streak. The specific gravity is 2.36.

Transparent and translucent wavellite crystal groups are found as secondary minerals in hydrothermal veins, in phosphate rocks and in some aluminous rocks. Fine crystals come from St Austell, Cornwall, and Barnstaple, Devon, in England, Dug Hill, Avant, Garland county, and from Hot Spring and Montgomery counties, both in Arkansas, USA. Wavellite is also found at Giessen and Langenstriegis in Germany, at Ouro Preto, Brazil, and at Llallagua, Bolivia. Remarkably, some cabochons have been cut from some Arkansas material, and these may reach several inches in length.

BRAZILIANITE

$$NaAl_3(PO_4)_2(OH)_4$$

Brazilianite (Minas Gerais, Brazil)

Named from its first and major location, brazilianite was discovered in the 1940s and described in 1945. The mineral forms large equant prismatic crystals of the monoclinic system which often appear spear-shaped; there is a perfect cleavage and faces are striated. Although its crystal size and clarity make it suitable for gem use, brazilianite is a soft 5.5 with a specific gravity of 2.9. The colour is pale to deep yellow, but it never attains the golden hue of yellow beryl, sapphire or even citrine. The lustre is notably glassy. The large size of the crystals indicates formation in pegmatite rocks, and most gem material has come from a pegmatite at Conselheiro Peña in the province of Minas Gerais, Brazil. Material of lower than gem quality has been discovered at the Palermo mine at Groton, New Hampshire, USA.

TORBERNITE

$$Cu(UO_2)(PO_4)_2.8–12H_2O$$

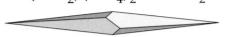

Torbernite forms thin square plates or small bipyramidal micaceous flakes of the tetragonal system. There is a perfect basal cleavage and the hardness is 2–2.5. The specific gravity is 3.2–3.6. It is yellowish-green to emerald-green with a pearly or vitreous lustre. It is translucent to transparent.

Torbernite is found in pegmatites and fine crystals are found at Gunnislake, Cornwall, England, and Mount Painter, South Australia. Very fine green crystals are found in Shaba Province, Zaire, and at the uranium-vanadium deposit at Mounana, Gabon.

Torbernite (North Carolina, USA)

AUTUNITE

$$Ca(UO_2)_2(PO_4)_2.10–12H_2O$$

Although autunite crystallizes in the tetragonal system, the thin tabular crystals (resembling those of torbernite) are slightly out of angle for the system; it is also found as crusts and aggregates. As with most uranium minerals, the colour is lemon- to sulphur-yellow, sometimes greenish-yellow to pale green; crystals are transparent to translucent with a vitreous lustre and yellowish streak. They show a strong yellowish-green fluorescence under ultra-violet radiation. Autunite has a hardness of 2–2.5 and a perfect cleavage. The specific gravity is 3.1. A dehydration product, meta-autunite, is less fluorescent.

Autunite is formed as a secondary mineral by the alteration of uraninite or other U-bearing minerals. It is to be found in weathered hydrothermal veins and pegmatites. Deposits include several places near Autun, Saone-et-Loire, France, Redruth and St Austell, Cornwall, England, and Rum Jungle, Northern Territory, Australia. The mineral is also found in the pegmatites at Hagendorf, Bavaria, and in several other places in Germany.

It is reported from the Katanga area of Zaire, from some South Dakota pegmatites and from North Carolina and New Mexico, USA.

VIVIANITE

$$Fe_3(PO_4)_2.8H_2O$$

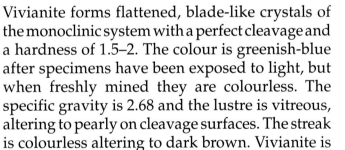

Vivianite forms flattened, blade-like crystals of the monoclinic system with a perfect cleavage and a hardness of 1.5–2. The colour is greenish-blue after specimens have been exposed to light, but when freshly mined they are colourless. The specific gravity is 2.68 and the lustre is vitreous, altering to pearly on cleavage surfaces. The streak is colourless altering to dark brown. Vivianite is easily soluble in acids and its flexible laminae are easy to recognize in the field.

It is found as a secondary mineral in the gossan of metallic ore deposits. Large crystals occur in the tin veins of Llallagua, Bolivia, and at St Agnes, Cornwall, England. It occurs in the pegmatites at Hagendorf, Bavaria, Germany. Fine specimens come from Leadville, Lake county, Colorado, and also from Lemhi county, Idaho in the USA, Cerro de Pasco in Peru, and Trepca in Yugoslavia.

Vivianite (Huanuni, Bolivia)

Autunite (Minas Gerais, Brazil)

LEGRANDITE

$$Zn_2(AsO_4)(OH).H_2O$$

Bright yellow legrandite crystals feature in many collections and some crystals have been found transparent enough to facet into very small gemstones. Legrandite crystallizes in the monoclinic system and forms radiating aggregates of prismatic crystals with a hardness of about 5 and a specific gravity of 3.9–4. Legrandite is transparent to translucent and is found in vugs in limonite. The finest crystals come from the Ojuela mine, Mapimi, Mexico.

LEFT Legrandite (Mapimi, Mexico)

FLUORAPATITE

$$Ca_5(PO_4)_3F$$

Fluorapatite is a member of the apatite group of minerals and provides interesting coloured crystals of the hexagonal system. The crystals are easy to recognize from the hexagonal cross-section and pyramidal termination. They have a hardness of 5 and specific gravity of 3.1–3.3. They show a vitreous lustre and a wide range of colours; probably the best known are the yellowish-green crystals from Durango, Mexico, and the violet crystals from Androscoggin county, Maine, USA. A blue variety is found in Brazil, where a greenish material, which may give a cat's-eye effect, is also to be found.

Purple crystals were once found in Greifenstein, Geyer, Germany, but no longer. Yellow hexagonal plates come from the famous mining area of Panasqueira, Portugal, and doubly-terminated blue-green prismatic crystals used to be found in England at Luxulyan, Cornwall, and the Bovey Tracey area of Devon. Emmelberg, in the Eifel area of Germany, provides some apatite and it has been found in Anhui, China.

Apatite shows a variety of fluorescent effects which depend upon variations in chemical composition for their different colours. Fluorescence is not a really diagnostic test for apatite but the crystals are probably some of the easiest to recognize in the field, especially in pegmatites which, with occurrences in other igneous rocks and in metamorphosed limestones, provide the host environment.

Fluorapatite (Maine, USA)

PYROMORPHITE

$$Pb_5(PO_4)_3Cl$$

Pyromorphite crystallizes in the hexagonal system, forming short hexagonal prisms with a prismatic cleavage and a hardness of 3.5–4. The specific gravity is 6.5–7.1 and the lustre resinous. The colour varies from a dark to a yellowish-green and the mineral is usually translucent.

Crystals are found as secondary minerals in the oxidation zone of lead ore deposits. Many crystals are cavernous. Fine examples come from Beresov in the USSR, Mies in Yugoslavia, Príbram in Czechoslovakia, and Clausthal, Bad Ems, Hofgrund and Pfahl in Germany. It occurs at Fieberbrunn, Tirol in Austria, and Les Farges, Ussel in France. In the British Isles pyromorphite is found at the Bwlch-Glas mine in central Wales and from Wheal Alfred, Phillack, Cornwall. A famous English locality for pyromorphite is Roughten Gill, Cumbria, and it also occurs at Leadhills, Lanarkshire in Scotland. Fine crystals are found on azurite at Grube Phillipseck, Munster, Taunus and Hesse in Germany. In Australia fine, bright yellow crystals are found at the Block 14 lease, Broken Hill, New South Wales. In the USA it is found at Phoenixville, Pennsylvania.

RIGHT Pyromorphite (Idaho, USA)

MIMETITE

$$Pb_5(AsO_4)_3Cl$$

Mimetite (Tsumeb, Namibia)

Mimetite gives some beautiful crystals in the monoclinic system; it forms some very well-shaped prisms, but more crystals are acicular or globular. Many are pseudo-hexagonal. There is a pyramidal cleavage and the hardness is 3.5–4. Specific gravity is 7.24. Mimetite is coloured bright orange to pale yellow and shows a vitreous lustre. Some crystals from Tsumeb, Namibia, show an orange-red fluorescence. Crystals are transparent to translucent. Mimetite is found as a secondary mineral in the oxidized zone of lead ore deposits. Fine, bright yellow crystals are found at Grube Clara, Wolfach in the Black Forest. The name campylite is given to orange-yellow, rounded crystals from British localities, including Alston Moor. In Australia fine orange crystals are reported from the Kintore opencast at Broken Hill, and green crystals from the Elura mine at Cobar, New South Wales. Mimetite is also found as 'wheatsheaf' growth at the Rowley mine, Painted Rock Mountains, Arizona. Deposits also occur in a number of places in Mexico, especially the Ojuela mine, Mapimi.

VANADINITE

Pb$_5$(VO$_4$)$_3$Cl

Orange-red crystals of vanadinite are sought by collectors for their startlingly fine colour and attractive shape. As a member of the hexagonal crystal system, vanadinite forms short to long prismatic crystals with a hardness of 2.75–3. The specific gravity is 6.8 and the lustre resinous to near-adamantine. The streak is white or yellowish and vanadinite is easily soluble in HNO$_3$. It is transparent to translucent. Vanadinite is found in the oxidation zone of lead ore deposits. The finest crystals occur in the USA – from the Red Cloud mine and the Old Yuma mine in Arizona, and from mines in New Mexico. Other occurrences include Wanlockhead, Scotland, where it occurs with smithsonite, Djebel Mahseur in Morocco, where large crystals are found, Beresov in the Urals, USSR, Tsumeb in Namibia, Bleiberg, Carinthia in Austria, Mies in Yugoslavia, and Los Lamentos in Mexico. Fine crystals from Mibladen, Morocco. Other recent US finds from the J. C. Holmes claim, Santa Cruz county, and the Hamburg mine, Yuma county, Arizona. It is also found in the Monti Livornesi, Tuscany, Italy, and at Gansu, China.

Vanadinite (Arizona, USA)

GYPSUM

CaSO$_4$.2H$_2$O

Gypsum crystallizes in the monoclinic system in which it forms thin to thick tabular crystals; swallow-tailed twins are common. There is a perfect cleavage and the hardness is 2. The specific gravity is 2.32. Gypsum may be colourless or show pale yellow, green or brown shades; it may be transparent to translucent. It gives a white streak and may show a greenish-white or yellow fluorescence and phosphorescence. It is sectile.

Gypsum is found in many places, chiefly in sedimentary deposits and in saline lakes, but also in the oxidized zones of ore deposits and in volcanic deposits. Rock-forming gypsum occurs in the Bellerophon strata of the Dolomites, Italy. Glassy crystals, found loose in clay beds, are known as selenite. Gypsum 'roses' are found at El Golea in the Sahara, Algeria, and good crystals come from Eisleben, Harz, Germany.

Gypsum (Zaragoza, Spain)

CELESTINE

$$SrSO_4$$

Pale blue to colourless crystals of celestine are found in sedimentary rocks, bedded gypsum deposits, cavities and veins in limestones and dolomites; it may also occur as a primary mineral in hydrothermal veins. A member of the orthorhombic crystal system, celestine forms thick to thin tabular crystals with a perfect cleavage or nodules and masses. The hardness is 3–3.5 and the specific gravity 3.97. The lustre is vitreous turning to pearly on cleavage surfaces.

Faceted stones have been cut from crystals found at Tsumeb, Namibia, and from Madagascar. Fine crystal groups are found at Agrigento, Sicily, and crystals also come from Yate and other areas near Bristol, England. Celestine has also been found in Austria – in the Leogang area and from the Katschberg road tunnel. Slender, yellowish crystals have been reported from Machow, Tarnobrzeg, Poland. In the United States fine, large blue crystals are found at Lampasas, Texas, and good crystals also come from a dolomite at Clay Center, Ohio.

Celestine (Ohio, USA)

ANGLESITE

PbSO$_4$

Anglesite (Tsumeb, Namibia)

Anglesite, named from the island of Anglesey, has occasionally been fashioned as a gemstone on account of its high lustre and dispersion; such material comes from Tsumeb, Namibia, or from Bou Azzer, Morocco. Anglesite is colourless to pale yellow and has a hardness of 2.5–3 with a specific gravity of 6.4. It is a member of the ortho-rhombic crystal system in which it forms tabular crystals with one direction of cleavage. It may show a weak yellow fluorescence under short-wave ultra-violet light. Anglesite is found as a secondary mineral from the oxidation of galena.

$BaSO_4$

In the field the heaviness of barite is a useful introductory test; indeed, it was once called 'heavy spar'. Crystallizing in the orthorhombic system, barite takes a wide number of forms, the commonest of which are thick or thin tabular crystals, often displaying a number of crystal faces. The hardness is 3–3.5 and there is a perfect cleavage . The specific gravity is 4.5 and the lustre vitreous to resinous. The crystals are transparent to translucent and the streak is white.

Although the fluorescence shown by some specimens is beautiful and interesting, it is not really useful as a diagnostic test; some crystals show an orange fluorescence and other crystals have a near-orange body colour caused by the inclusion of hematite or sulphide minerals.

Barite is the commonest barium-bearing mineral; it is found as a gangue (non-ore) mineral in metalliferous veins of hydrothermal origin, being particularly characteristic of medium to low temperatures. It is often found with fluorite, calcite, siderite, dolomite, quartz, galena and other minerals. It is also found in limestones and other sedimentary rocks in which it forms veins or lenses.

Good specimens of barite are found in the mining area of north-east England, particularly Alston Moor, Frizington, and Cleator Moor. Several places in Cornwall also produce barite, including Wheal Mary Ann, Menheniot. Other deposits occur in the German mining area of Freiberg and from Grube Clara, Schwarzwald. Yellow crystals are found at Grube Machow, Tarnobrzeg, Poland. Fine blue crystals come from Stoneham and Sterling, Colorado, and what are probably the finest gem-quality crystals also come from the USA where the Elk Creek deposit in South Dakota still produces material. 'Desert Roses' formed from barite and sand are found in a number of places in Oklahoma and Kansas.

Barite (Elk Creek, South Dakota, USA)

CROCOITE

PbCrO$_4$

Magnificent orange crystals of crocoite from the Dundas area of Tasmania feature in many mineral collections. They occur at the former Adelaide, West Comet, Dundas Extension mines, no longer in production, with chrome cerussite, massicot and other minerals. Crocoite is a member of the monoclinic system and forms characteristically elongated prismatic crystals with smooth, brilliant faces. There is a distinct cleavage and the mineral is sectile. The hardness is 2.5–3 and the specific gravity 5.99. Crocoite shows an adamantine to vitreous lustre with an orange-yellow streak; crystals are transparent.

Crocoite is a secondary mineral found in the gossan (rock rich in silica and iron oxides) of mineral deposits and associated with pyromorphite, cerussite and sometimes wulfenite and vanadinite. It was first reported from the Beresov district in the Urals, USSR, and also occurs at Rezbanya, Romania. In addition, good crystals are reported from Goyabeira, Minas Gerais, Brazil. In the USA it is found with wulfenite at the Darwin mines, Inyo county, California, and at the Mammoth mine, Pinal county, Arizona, with wulfenite and vanadinite. It is also reported from Zimbabwe.

Crocoite (Dundas, Tasmania)

WULFENITE

$$PbMoO_4$$

Wulfenite (San Pedro Corralitos, Mexico)

Wulfenite forms square tabular crystals of the tetragonal system which are sought by collectors because of their orange-yellow or bright red colour. The hardness is 2.75–3 and the specific gravity 6.5–7. The lustre is resinous to adamantine and the streak is white. Wulfenite is soluble in concentrated sulphuric acid.

It is found in the oxidized zones of lead and molybdenum deposits. Very fine crystals come from the Red Cloud mine, Yuma county, and the Rowley mine, Painted Mountain, both in Arizona, USA. Deposits also occur at Bleiberg, Carinthia in Austria, Mies in Yugoslavia, and Chah-Karbose in Iran. Thin yellow plates are found in Sonora, Mexico, where they occur with orange mimetite at the San Francisco mine. Small, bright yellow crystals have been found at the Whim Well mine, Whim Creek Gold Field, Western Australia. Translucent crystals of good quality come from the lead mines at Loudville, Massachusetts, USA, and from the lead slags at Laurium, Greece. Finds are also reported from the Bwlch-Glas mine, central Wales, and from Montevecchio, Sardinia, Italy.

SCHEELITE

CaWO$_4$

Scheelite (Cochise county, Arizona, USA)

Scheelite can be an important ore of tungsten but is also sought by mineral collectors and has sometimes been cut as a gemstone. It crystallizes in the tetragonal crystal system, forming octahedra or occurring as masses. There are three distinct directions of cleavage and the hardness is 4.5–5. Scheelite is colourless to yellow with a vitreous to adamantine lustre and specific gravity of 5.9-6.3 It is translucent to transparent and gives a bright blue-white fluorescence under short-wave ultra-violet radiation; this feature is used in prospecting the contact metamorphic deposits, hydrothermal veins and pegmatites in which scheelite occurs. It can also be found in placer deposits.

Fine crystals found in Sonora, Mexico, can be of gem quality and are coloured orange-brown; similar finds have been made in Tong Wha, Korea. Other localities include Bishop and Atolia in California, USA, the Ramsley mine, Sticklepath, Devon in England, Bruchgraben, Hollersbachtal in Austria, and Tavetsch and Iragna, Ticino in Switzerland. It has been reported from Hunan and Liaoning, China.

WOLFRAMITE

$(Fe,Mn)WO_4$

Wolframite crystallizes in the monoclinic system, forming black blades which are usually found in white vein quartz. It may also be found as large groups of subparallel crystals or as granular masses. There is a perfect cleavage and the hardness is 4–4.5. Wolframite is frequently twinned and has a submetallic lustre. The specific gravity is 7.1–7.5. The streak is black to reddish-brown.

Wolframite is an important ore of tungsten and is found in quartz-rich veins or in pegmatitic veins associated with granite intrusive rocks. It may also occur in high-temperature hydrothermal veins or in contact metamorphic deposits. Fine crystals are to be found at Panasqueira, Portugal, at various places in Cornwall, England, including St Michael's Mount. Also at Tong Wha in Korea, Guangdong in China, and at many other places throughout the world.

LEFT Wolframite on quartz (Ancash, Peru)

PART THREE

DEPOSITS

Some of the world's best-known sources of fine mineral and gem crystals are described. There are, of course, a great number of interesting deposits, but the ones described are for the most part reasonably accessible, as far as any mineral deposits can be.

Wind-eroded sandstone gives rise to these distinctive structures in Monument Valley, Utah, USA.

Franklin and Sterling Hill, New Jersey, USA

This zinc-producing area is about 50 miles/80km north-west of New York City and has produced 250 different mineral species, some 25 of which have not been found elsewhere to date. The area is particularly celebrated for its fluorescent minerals and for deep red, transparent crystals of zincite, a few of which have been faceted as gemstones. The main ores of zinc at this locality are franklinite and zincite. There is a fine mineral museum at Franklin where the veins were exhausted and the mine closed in 1954. Sterling Hill was working in the mid-1980s.

Cave-in-Rock, Hardin County, Illinois, USA

The Hardin county area houses the main fluorite-producing mines in the United States. Vein ore bodies are found in fissures in a complex system of faults. In early mining days fine crystals of fluorite came from vein deposits in the Rosiclare district. Later, after the exhaustion of ore bodies in the 1950s, bedded deposits were found to the north of Cave-in-Rock. Crystals were formed by a reaction between calcium carbonate in the underlying limestone and fluorine-bearing solutions. Very large yellow and purple crystals came from the Rosiclare Mine; straw-yellow barite crystals on purple fluorite are recorded from the Gaskins Mine in Pope County, and the North Green Mine has produced very large sphalerite crystals on yellow fluorite. The Minerva mine has produced

Linarite (Mammoth mine, Tiger, Arizona, USA)

fluorite in many colours with very fine pale yellow rhombohedra of witherite, and has also produced the first recorded American occurrence of alstonite.

The Tri-State District, USA

The three states are Kansas, Missouri and Oklahoma. The mines of the Joplin and Sweetwater districts of Missouri have produced some of the finest galena crystals ever found. Also recorded are small but beautiful transparent, bright red sphalerite, chalcopyrite on dolomite, sphalerite and galena and hemimorphite pseudomorphs after calcite.

Butte, Montana, USA

Gold was reported from Butte in the 1860s but the area is more famous for its crystals of covelline, pyrite, rhodochrosite and enargite. Covelline was found as hexagonal plates, particularly from the Leonard Mine. The area became well celebrated for its very large deposits of copper, lead and zinc and is one of the most significant copper deposits known.

Crystal Peak, Colorado, USA

Here the country rock is granite penetrated by pegmatite dykes. Fine crystals of amazonite feldspar, smoky quartz and amethyst, fluorite, topaz, goethite, cassiterite and phenakite are among the minerals reported, although amazonite is the best known.

Mammoth Mine, Tiger, Arizona, USA

Begun as a gold mine in the 1880s, the Mammoth site later became famous for base metal sulphides and vanadium. Crystals of lead compounds – leadhillite, linarite, wulfenite, phosgenite and copper minerals dioptase and azurite – are among the very fine specimen materials produced by the mine. Specimens of micromount size are particularly beautiful; yellow fluorite is also found and fine twinned cerussite with wulfenite.

Red Cloud Mine, Yuma, Arizona, USA

This is the classic location for superb red crystals of wulfenite, with small crystals of vanadinite, willemite, cerussite, pyrolusite, quartz and fluorite, the last two sometimes intergrown. In the 1980s it was hoped that the mine could be

Wulfenite (Red Cloud mine, Yuma county, Arizona, USA)

reopened so that more fine wulfenite crystals might be found there.

Copper Queen Mine, Bisbee, Arizona, USA

Copper outcrops were first reported in 1877, silver having already been noticed. Botryoidal azurite and tufts of malachite crystals were notable specimens from the mine, as well as crystal groups of cuprite cubes up to 0.75in/2cm on edge. About 214 different species have been reported from the mine but the best known must be the azurmalachite combinations. The mine is open as a tourist attraction and there is a mining museum.

Himalaya Mine, Mesa Grande, California, USA

In much the same way that tourmaline crystals were first discovered at Mount Mica, Maine, children were apparently the first to notice brightly coloured crystals at Mesa Grande, 40 miles/64km north-east of San Diego. Some of the crystals were coloured bright red, green or blue and were finally identified as tourmaline by a New York jeweller. The source was a pegmatite dyke and for a number of years the mine produced tourmaline, quartz and fine pink-orange morganite beryl from 400 individual dykes.

Pala District, San Diego County, California, USA

The pegmatite dykes of the Pala district have produced very fine crystals of tourmaline and kunzite, with quartz and cleavelandite. Again, these come from mines in pegmatite. By far the most important mines of all have been the Pala Chief, Stewart Lithia mine, Tourmaline King and Tourmaline Queen. Crystals of a 'shocking' pink are especially typical of this area.

Mapimi, Durango, Mexico

Silver ores were first discovered in this area during the late sixteenth century, and for many years the Ojuela mine in particular was one of Mexico's greatest locations for minerals. Finds include adamite, wulfenite, aurichalcite, white crystals of hemimorphite, azurite and, probably most famous of all, yellow crystals of legrandite. Rarer minerals include dark red carminite and pale yellow paradamite.

Mont St Hilaire, Quebec, Canada

The area about 19 miles/30km east of Montreal is mined for a nepheline syenite rock, which is used as an aggregate in concrete. The nepheline syenite is altered by magmatic intrusions with some pegmatite dykes. In these dykes a number of rare mineral species have been found and a book published in 1989 – *Monteregian Treasures* by Mandarino and Anderson – gives the first full monographic account of the often micromount-sized minerals. Collecting is possible in the quarries only through the good offices of the Ecole Polytechnique of Montreal. Among the many beautiful and rare species are orange serandite, red manganeptunite, genthelvite of a pale straw yellow and forming tetrahedra, gem-quality yellow zircon, ekanite (only previously reported

Adamite (Mapimi, Durango, Mexico)

from Sri Lanka), yellow wulfenite and orange-red crystals of labuntsovite. Perhaps the most attractive combination is orange serandite on white analcime, but many more minerals remain to be identified and others to be discovered.

Jeffrey Mine, Asbestos, Quebec, Canada
The deposit lies about 100 miles/160km east of Quebec and was first worked for chrysotile, an asbestos mineral. It occurs in a stockwork of veins in a serpentine, fissures in the serpentine housing a variety of beautifully crystallized minerals. Most famous are the superb and virtually perfect grossular crystals which can reach 1in/3cm across and which occur in orange, colourless and green varieties. Forms are combinations of rhombic dodecahedron and icositetrahedron. Some smaller grossular crystals are emerald green and are found with white crystals of prehnite. Also among the minerals recorded are green vesuvianite crystals with deep pink or purple terminations.

Muzo Mine, Colombia
With the mines at Chivor, the Muzo mines form one of the two greatest locations for emerald so far known. The Muzo mines are 93 miles/150km north of Bogota and comprise thick layers of dark shales shot through with calcite veins containing the emerald crystals. Gemmologists can recognize faceted stones cut from Muzo crystals by their inclusions of minute parisite.

Proustite (Chanarcillo, Chile)

Chanarcillo, Chile
In 1832 a prospector found high-grade silver ore in the Andes area of northern Chile and a mine was eventually established at a spot below Chanarcillo Mountain. The Dolores Tercera mine became famous for its other minerals, especially for proustite, some crystals of which reached 2.5in/6cm in length. Other fine crystals of argentite (acanthite) on calcite, pyrargyrite and stephanite were found, as well as arborescent and wire silver. Little if any mining takes place in the area now.

Topaz mines, Minas Gerais, Brazil
Several mines west of the town of Ouro Preto produce some of the world's finest topaz crystals. Three areas have been identified: Dom Bosco, Rodrigo Silva and Saramenha. Crystals are found in a kaolinite clay penetrated by quartz veins and also in sedimentary iron formations made of hematite and silica (locally known as itabirite). No trace apparently exists of the pegmatites from which the crystals presumably originated. Some sherry-coloured crystals from the area are heated to give a stable pink colour.

Grossular (Asbestos, Quebec, Canada)

Golconda Mines, Minas Gerais, Brazil

This area, about 21 miles/34km north-west of the town of Governador Valadares, has produced much of Brazil's finest tourmaline, but it is by no means the only tourmaline-producing area. Aquamarine, reddish-brown spessartine, minute yellow microlite, pink beryl (morganite) and hydroxyl-herderite are also found. The minerals occur in pegmatite pockets.

Broken Hill, New South Wales, Australia

Something like 180 different mineral species have been found at what was first noticed as a jagged outcrop. Tin was the mineral originally sought but the discovery of silver-lead ores made the area one of the richest of its kind in the world. Among the minerals reported are fine crystals of rhodonite, cerussite, fine dodecahedra of spessartine, pyrrhotite altered to pyrargyrite, arborescent groups of elongated silver crystals, twinned crystals of green orthoclase, blue-green smithsonite, bluish-green apatite and fine crystals of azurite. Among rarer species are the bright yellowish-orange crystals of anglesite and emerald-green crystals of brochantite.

Dundas, Tasmania

The Adelaide mine was established in the late nineteenth century in a silver-lead district near Dundas. It is particularly famous for its magnificent red crystals of crocoite, the finest examples known. They come from the ore body, which is composed of ferromagnesian gossan. It is generally thought that no more mining will now take place in the area and the town of Dundas has already been deserted.

Mogok, Burma

This area in Upper Burma has produced the world's finest rubies and red spinels which are now found by working the byon, a gravelly, gem-bearing layer into which the gem crystals settled on the weathering out of their host rock of metamorphosed limestone. Also in the byon are pebbles of blue cordierite, blue apatite, phenakite, garnets, blue sillimanite and yellow danburite. Interestingly, the red spinel crystals, though softer than ruby, maintain a better crystal shape during their long history. At the present time the area is scarcely accessible for a number of reasons and

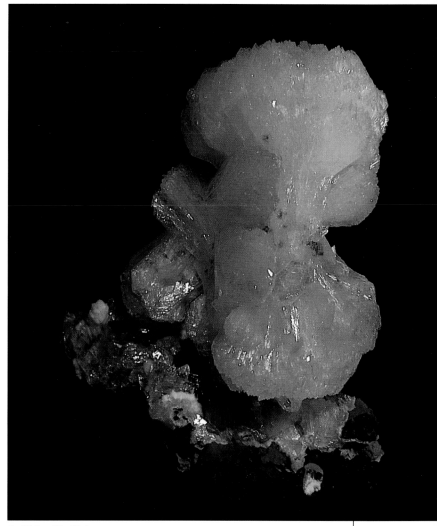

Stilbite (India)

many of the finest crystals are said to be smuggled out to Thailand. Stones offered at state auctions in Rangoon are said to be of inferior quality.

Deccan Basalt, India

The Deccan basalt covers a very large area indeed of western India and in the lava flows are many crystal-bearing vugs created by dissolved gases. Three particular areas – Nasik, Bombay and Poona – are especially celebrated for very fine crystals of green apophyllite and for varieties of zeolites, including mesolite, stilbite and heulandite. The now famous Jewel Tunnel was constructed in the early part of the twentieth century and traverses a volcanic basalt between Bombay and Poona. At the time of its construction it was filled with crystals which glittered on the walls. In time, however, the crystals were mostly obscured by sooty deposits. The basalts are mined today mainly for roadstone.

Taita Hills, Kenya

In the early 1970s geologists noticed that Precambrian metamorphic graphite-bearing gneisses occurred in the hills of south-eastern Kenya. As this type of formation contained gem minerals in Tanzania on the other side of the border, the Kenyan deposits were prospected. Chips of bright green grossular were traced to a belt of graphite schist. The crystals, though fairly small as a rule and not well-formed, showed a very fine, dark emerald-green colour and have since become known as tsavolite, a trade name alluding to the Tsavo National Park in which the locality lies. The grossular occurs in large porphyroblasts which have been called 'potatoes' and which are very easily shattered. Fine ruby corundum has also been found in the Tsavo game preserve.

Merelani Mine, Arusha, Tanzania

This mine is so far the only known source of the superb blue 'tanzanite' variety of zoisite. This was first found in 1966 in the Usumburu mountains bordering the Umba Valley of northern Tanzania. The crystals, often well-formed, are found in a tough metamorphosed rock and are strongly pleochroic. When heated, one of the colours becomes a magnificent sapphire-blue. Crystals have never really been in plentiful supply, but they can reach large sizes and there are constant rumours that the supply is exhausted; such stories are common where gem minerals are concerned.

Anjanabonoina Mine, Antsirabe, Madagascar

Madagascar's wealth of fine gem minerals was known by the end of the nineteenth century, and the Anjanabonoina deposit was discovered in 1900. It lies about 40 miles/65km south of Antsirabe and the pegmatite mine was worked for tourmaline, kunzite spodumene, amazonite, spessartine, danburite and other minerals. Further exploration of the by-then deserted mine took place in 1970 when more material was discovered, enabling mining to recommence in 1972. Particularly famous are the tourmaline sections displaying different colours and the exceptionally fine deep rose morganite beryl.

Tsumeb Mine, Namibia

This mine is probably the greatest on earth in respect of the different mineral species found, many of very fine quality. The copper outcrop was discovered in 1892 and with further prospecting mining was in progress by 1900. At least 150 different species are found at Tsumeb, of which about 25 have been found nowhere else. Many species known from other localities occur here in a much greater variety of colours. Along with copper and lead are deposits of gallium, cadmium, vanadium, germanium, which also play a part in the formation of unusual species. Large azurite crystals have been found recently at considerable depth – below 4000 feet/1220 metres.

Panasqueira, Portugal

Panasqueira is about 211 miles/340km north-east of Lisbon, and Fundao is the nearest settlement. The mine is worked for tin and tungsten, and very fine crystals of wolframite and apatite are found, the latter being tabular, green and lavender. Fine groups of arsenopyrite crystals are also reported. Mining here has gone on since Roman times.

Bourg d'Oisans, France

The mines are in the Dauphiné region of eastern France and mining first began when gold was found on the surface in the late eighteenth century. The area is famous for very fine quartz crystals as well as for fine chalcopyrite and barite. The quartz crystals frequently display a type of twinning once known as gardette twinning after the mine La Gardette; later these twins became known as Japan twins.

Azurite (Tsumeb, Namibia)

Apatite (Panasqueira, Portugal)

Calcite (Cumbria, England)

Egremont Mining District, Cumbria, England

This area is especially famous for its barite crystal groups, although iron was the mineral particularly sought in this north-west corner of England. Classic crystals of mimetite and pyromorphite come from Roughton Gill and Drygill but some of the finest mineral specimens come from a few mines about 44 miles/70km south-west of Carlisle. The Cleator Moor and Frizington areas produce turquoise-blue fluorite (from the Florence mine), golden barite (from Dalmellington), and blue barite and green fluorite (from the Mowbray mine). The Florence mine was taken over by the British Steel Corporation and renamed the Beckermet mine. Kidney ore is found there interlaced with calcite.

Northern Pennine Orefield, England

This area is one of the world's great sources of fine fluorite crystals and although very few of the mines are still in operation, some crystals are recovered from time to time. Green and purple or amber colours are to be found, often in association with chalcopyrite. Yellow fluorite on needle-like quartz crystals are classic specimens from the area. The mines have been worked for lead since early times (at least since the twelfth century).

Herodsfoot Mine, Cornwall, England

This mine is the classic location for the large, cogwheel crystals of bournonite. Worked for lead and silver, the mine dates from the eighteenth century. Fine crystals of bournonite and iridescent tetrahedrite were found in the upper levels of the South Herodsfoot mine in the early 1860s and good crystals of calcite, pyrite, dolomite and chalcopyrite were also found. The best examples of tetrahedrite and bournonite are in the Natural History Museum, London.

Grimsel Area, Berne, Switzerland

This is the area in which the finest pink fluorites are found. The exact locality is in difficult country north of the Grimsel-Andermatt road. During work on the tunnels for a hydroelectric scheme, very fine pink fluorites were found at Bratschi. Fine examples sit on quartz crystals. The largest octahedron of fluorite to be found in Switzerland is pale green and measures 6in/16cm on an edge; it was found at Sommerloch during the construction of an underground power station. Even larger crystals have apparently been found in sedimentary deposits in the northern Alps.

Lengenbach Quarries, Valais, Switzerland

The minerals of the Binntal are world-famous and up to 70 species have been identified from the main site, the Lengenbach quarry. Specimens are particularly beautiful, though small, and most are sulphosalts and sulphates recovered from the white granular dolomite rock. The quarries are mined by several academic institutions and are not open to general and amateur collectors. However, the dumps are available to all and crystal specimens can sometimes be purchased in the local vicinity.

Rutile (Turpen Alps, Binntal, Switzerland)

Knappenwand, Untersulzbachtal, Austria
This locality is famous for its fine crystals of epidote, which occur with byssolite or apatite, calcite or feldspar. Most of the epidote is dark green to black but pale yellow crystals are also reported. Deposits were first discovered in 1865 and the site is now worked by the Department of Mineralogy of the Natural History Museum, Vienna, Austria.

Kongsberg, Norway
Silver was first exposed here in the seventeenth century and the mine has been open in some way since that time. Today it can be visited via a narrow-gauge railway extending into some of the old workings. The mountain in which the workings are situated contains gneisses, and east-west bands of calcite often contain silver. There is a most interesting mine museum on the site.

Freiberg, Germany
Silver was first discovered at Freiberg in the twelfth century and the Bergakademie (School of Mines) was founded in 1765. Fine crystals came especially from the Himmelfahrt mine and fine specimens of pyrargyrite from the Himmelsfurst mine, south-west of Freiberg. The area is known for a variety of fine mineral crystals. These include yellow fluorite cubes from the Halsbrucke mine, acanthite from the Brand mine, arsenopyrite, tetrahedrite, calcite, dolomite, siderite, barite in various colours and proustite. The Bergakademie houses a fine collection of minerals from the area.

St Andreasberg, Germany
The mine area lies in the Harz Mountains and was a centre for lead-silver ores from the twelfth century onwards. Very fine specimens came from several of the mines, including green, yellow and blue fluorite, variously coloured barite, calcite, malachite and quartz as interesting crystals, tetrahedrite, datolite, stilbite, analcime, smithsonite and many sulphosalts; these include pyrargyrite, stephanite and polybasite. Pink apophyllite crystals were also found.

Príbram, Czechoslovakia
Príbram is about 37 miles/60km south-west of Prague and silver has been mined in the area from the thirteenth century onwards. Fine crystals from some of the mines include columnar pyrargyrite, proustite, polybasite, stephanite, boulangerite and amethyst. About 110 different species have been reported. Uranium has been discovered in recent years.

Wieliczka, Poland
This famous salt mine is close to the city of Krakow and is the most spectacular salt mine in the world. Still producing, it began working at least as far back as the thirteenth century, from which time underground work began. Most of the fine crystals occur deep in the mine, much of which is a museum of amazing quality. Most crystals are water-clear and some have reddish or yellowish tints from impurities. Some have measured 16in/40cm on an edge.

Mursinka, Sverdlovsk, USSR
Unfortunately this area is not accessible to visitors, but fine crystals of topaz, smoky quartz, very fine red and pink tourmaline, different colours of beryl and amethyst were found in pegmatites about 75 miles/120km north of Sverdlovsk in the Ural Mountains. At the Tokovaya mines at Sverdlovsk, pegmatites have yielded up phenakite, chrysoberyl (especially very fine alexandrite), amethyst and topaz.

MUSEUMS

Canada
Department of Mineralogy, Royal Ontario
Museum, Toronto, Ontario

Czechoslovakia
Katedra Mineralogie a Krystalografie,
Univerzity Komenskeho, Bratislava
Katedra Mineralogie a Petrografie, Univerzity
Purkyne, Kotlarska 2, Brno
Moravian Museum, Department of Mineralogy,
Namesti 25 unora 8, Brno
Sleezske Muzeum, Vitzneho unora 35, Opava

Germany
Museum für Naturkunde, Humboldt
Universitat, Berlin
Staatliches Museum für Mineralogie und
Geologie, Augustusstrasse 2, Dresden
Bergakademie Freiberg, Sektion
Geowissenschaften, Freiberg, Saxony
Mineralogical Museum, Division of Mineralogy,
Section of Chemistry, Martin Luther
Universitat, Halle/Saale
Goethe Nationalmuseum, National Forschungs
und Gedenkstatten der klassichen Deutschen
Literatur, Am Frauenplan 1, Weimar

Poland
Academy of Mining and Metallurgy, Institute of
Mineralogy, al Mickiewicza 30, Krakow
Geological Institute, Rakowiecka 4, Warsaw
Ziemu Museum, Polish Academy of Sciences,
Warsaw

United Kingdom
Natural History Museum, Cromwell Road,
London
Mineral Collection, Department of Geology,
University of Leicester, University Road,
Leicester
Sedgwick Museum, University of Cambridge,
Department of Earth Sciences, Downing
Street, Cambridge
University Museum, Parks Road, Oxford

United States
American Museum of Natural History, New
York City, New York
Field Museum of Natural History, Chicago,
Illinois
Harvard College Museum, Cambridge,
Massachusetts
Los Angeles County Museum, Los Angeles,
California
National Museum of Natural History,
Smithsonian Institution, Washington DC
Pennsylvania Academy of Science Museum,
Philadelphia, Pennsylvania

USSR
Chernyshow Central Research Geological
Museum, Sredny Prospect 74, Leningrad
A.E. Fersman Mineralogical Museum, USSR
Academy of Science, Leninsky Prospect 18–2,
Moscow V–71
Geological Mineralogical Museum, Grozny Oil
Institute, Ordzhonikideze Square 100,
Grozny
Geological Museum, Institute of Mineral
Resources, Ukrainian Ministry of Geology,
Kirov Prospect 47/2, Simferopol
Geological Museum, Ukrainian Academy of
Sciences, Lenin str 15, Kiev
Mineralogical Collection, Institute of
Mineralogy, Sadovnicheskaya Nabereszhnaya
71, Moscow
Mineralogical Museum, Lvov State University,
Stcherbakov str 4, Lvov
Mineralogical Museum, Moscow Geological
Prospecting Institute, Marx Prospect 18,
Moscow
Mining Institute of Leningrad, 21 Line 2,
Leningrad
Museum of the Geological Institute, Kola
Academy of Science, Fersman Str 14, Apatity
Museum of Earth Sciences, Moscow State
University, MGU Leninskie Gory, Moscow
Ural Geological Museum, Sverdlovsk Mining
Institute, Kuibyshve str 30, Sverdlovsk

BIBLIOGRAPHY

The mineralogist would serve his or her needs very satisfactorily with a bookshelf of basic treatises on general inorganic chemistry, thermo-chemistry, elementary physics and algebra. A reasonable knowledge of the behaviour of cations and anions in a variety of temperature, pressure and compositional regimes is indispensable. Since crystallography and crystal chemistry are the foundations of mineralogy, group theory is an essential topic and here lies the importance of algebraic techniques. As for good treatises in mineralogy, there are none. The entire science badly needs revision; indeed, it should be re-named inorganic natural products chemistry (Paul Brian Moore, *Mineralogical Record*, volume 9, issue 1, 1978).

Professor Moore's future-looking article notwithstanding, there is no doubt that existing ways of examining minerals have generated a great deal of literature, most of it taxonomic and relatively little of it dealing with the chemistry of minerals. However, most of it is scattered among a wide variety of journals covering non-mineral science. There are not very many minerals, so there are not, compared with other sciences, very many large, standard monographs. Literature contained in geological survey reports takes the place of monographs, and there are only one or two journals entirely devoted to the subject. So far there is no up-to-date general mineralogy, let alone one based on Professor Moore's concepts, and few countries or states have their own mineralogies. (That for the United Kingdom was first published in 1858 and reprinted with supplementary lists of minerals in 1977.) For details of new and discredited species the mine-ralogist should really subscribe to more than one journal.

Demand for mineralogical literature may come from field collectors, economic geologists and prospectors. For this group the mere identification of places is so daunting a task that abstracting services and databases need to be combined as a single search tool and used in conjunction with monograph literature. Geological maps are also vital and institutions holding significant collec-tions should be familiar to serious workers. Older literature is still very important for details of forgotten locations, changes of place-name and records of minerals whose whereabouts may now be lost. (Such specimens may come to assume great importance in the light of later research.)

The serious worker, therefore, needs access to libraries which can provide all the elements listed above. In practice this means the national library, the main geological survey library or a large university library. Very large national and univer-sity libraries, such as the British Library, the Bodleian Library, Cambridge University Library, the Library of Congress and the State Lenin Library, will cover the whole world, not merely their own country. Access to some of these may not be easily available to amateurs and, once in, there is still the task of knowing what to look for. The list below gives some of the books needed by the mineralogist. Note: the major comprehensive descriptive works always list minerals in chemical order. If you come across one of these multi-volume books, make sure you obtain the volume with the index.

Textbooks

Bibliography and Index of Geology, American Geological Institute, Falls Church, Va., 1934–. This is also available on the GeoRef database (see On-line Services).

Bishop, A.C. *An Outline of Crystal Morphology*, Hutchinson, London, 1967.

Bloss, F.D. *Crystallography and Crystal Chemistry*, Holt, Rinehart and Winston, New York, 1971. A useful overview.

Chalmers, R.O. *Australian Rocks, Minerals and Gemstones*, Angus & Robertson, Sydney, 1967. The best guide to Australian gems and minerals.

Dana, E.S. *A Textbook of Mineralogy*, fourth edition revised by W.E. Ford, John Wiley, New York and London, 1932. Still valuable for its comprehensiveness, but the details of mineral chemistry are now unreliable.

Dana, J.D. and E.S. *The System of Mineralogy*, first edition, 1837, seventh edition by Palache, Berman and Frondel, John Wiley, New York and London, 1944. A set of supplements to the fourth edition appeared in the *American Journal of Science*, 1855–62. The fifth edition was published in 1868 and had three appendices; the sixth was published in 1892 with appendices in 1899 and 1909. The seventh edition is still incomplete, lacking the volume on silicates. Prospective mineralogists need to get hold of at least the sixth edition, but be warned – it is very expensive and hard to find.

Deer, W.A., Howie, R.A. and Zussman, J. *Rock-forming Minerals*, second edition, three volumes published so far. Longman Scientific and Technical, Harlow, 1978–. Mineral relationships are now seen as very important clues to rock and mineral formation. A vital work for the study of thermodynamic properties of minerals and of phase equilibria.

Embrey, Peter and Fuller, John, eds. *A Manual of New Mineral Names, 1892–1978*, Natural History Museum, London, 1980. Incorporates the lists of minerals published more or less annually in the *Mineralogical Magazine* from 1897 to 1978, including discredited and trade names, mistranslations and misspellings.

Evans, R.C. *An Introduction to Crystal Chemistry*, second edition, Cambridge University Press, Cambridge, 1964.

Fleischer, Michael. *Glossary of Mineral Species*, *Mineralogical Record*, Tucson, Arizona, 1971–. A convenient way of keeping up to date with the growing number of mineral descriptions approved by the Commission on New Minerals and Mineral Names of the International Mineralogical Association as first published in one of the established mineral journals.

Frye, Keith. *The Encyclopedia of Mineralogy*, Hutchinson Ross, Stroudsberg, 1981. Hard to equal for comprehensiveness; it includes a bibliography, and further references appear within some of the main entries.

Frye, Keith. *Modern Mineralogy*, Prentice-Hall, Inc., Englewood Cliffs, New Jersey, 1974. A

useful guide, but not for the amateur.

Goldschmidt, V. *Atlas der Krystallformen*, Carl Winters Universitätsbuchhandlung, Heidelberg, 1916–23. An eighteen-part work with diagrams of thousands of crystals that gives all mineral details published up to 1916 and which is therefore valuable for tracking down species whose type material may have been lost.

Hey, Max. *An Index of Mineral Species and Varieties Arranged Chemically*, Natural History Museum, London, 1962. Invaluable for day-to-day desk or bench use; this lists all the names ever used (discredited and current) and even includes pronunciation help. The chemical arrangement, explained in the preface to the book, is easy to follow and there is a full index. Entries also include references to *Mineralogical Abstracts* or other sources wherever possible. A new edition is expected shortly.

Hintze, Carl. *Handbuch der Mineralogie* (11 volumes, Walter de Gruyter, Berlin, 1889–1971). An all-important book enormously rich in locality information.

Hurlbut, C.S. and Klein, C.K. (after J.D. Dana), *Manual of Mineralogy*, John Wiley, New York, 1985. Smaller and easier to understand than Bloss.

Klockmann, Friedrich. *Lehrbuch der Mineralogie*, Enke Verlag, Stuttgart, 1978. A useful German monograph.

O'Donoghue, Michael. *Encyclopedia of Minerals and Gemstones*, Orbis, London, 1976. Contains numerous photographs, many of minerals from European locations. Parts of this book have been issued separately.

O'Donoghue, Michael. *The Literature of Mineralogy*, Science Reference and Information Service of the British Library, London, 1986. A useful book for finding your way around specialist libraries.

Phillips, F.C. *An Introduction to Crystallography*, Longmans, Green and Co., London, 1971. A very good treatment of the subject.

Roberts, W.L., Campbell, T.J. and Weber, J. *Encyclopedia of Minerals*, Van Nostrand Reinhold, New York, 1990. Contains a number of colour photographs.

Sinkankas, John. *Gemstone and Mineral Data*

Book, Winchester Press, New York, 1972. An unequalled text for beginners.

Sinkankas, John. *Prospecting for Gemstones and Minerals*, Van Nostrand Reinhold, New York and London, 1970. Contains information on the recognition of gem-bearing geological formations, handling specimens and so on.

Spencer, L.J. *Catalogue of Topographical Mineralogies and Regional Bibliographies* (*Mineralogical Magazine*, London, 28, pages 303–32, 1948). Despite its age, this is still a useful reference tool.

Winchell, A.N. and H. *Elements of Optical Mineralogy*, fourth edition, John Wiley, New York, 1951. The best work in this field.

Wood, D.N., Hardy, J.E. and Harvey, A.P. *Information Sources in the Earth Sciences*, Bowker-Saur, London, 1989. Another useful book for finding your way through the available written material.

Mineral Identification

It is still possible for the amateur to identify many mineral specimens, though the majority of determinations are now carried out with the help of X-ray techniques. There are several useful guides.

Bloss, F.D. *An Introduction to the Methods of Optical Crystallography*, Holt, Rinehart and Winston, New York, 1961.

Larsen, E.S. and Berman, H. *Microscopic Determination of the Non-opaque Minerals*, Bulletin 848 of the United States Geological Survey, 1934. Together with Bloss, probably still the best known.

Mitchell, Richard S. *Mineral Names – What Do They Mean?*, Van Nostrand Reinhold, New York, 1979. The best book, which has been drawn upon for the present work.

Troger, E. *Optical Determination of Rock-forming Minerals*, Part 1, Schweizerbart, Stuttgart, 1979. A translation of Part 1 of the fourth German edition with which, for the present, it will have to be used.

Winchell. A.N. *Elements of Optical Mineralogy*, John Wiley and Sons, Inc., New York, 1937. Still useful, despite its age.

Regional Mineralogies

These are too numerous to list here in full (see O'Donoghue, op. cit.). However, the titles below, all by J.D. Ridge and published by the Geological Society of America, are worth finding.

Selected Bibliographies of Hydrothermal and Magmatic Mineral Deposits, Memoirs no. 75, 1958.

Annotated Bibliographies of Mineral Deposits in the Western Hemisphere, Memoirs no. 131, 1972. This is a revision and expansion of the above.

Annotated Bibliographies of Mineral Deposits in Africa, Asia (exclusive of the USSR) and Australasia, Pergamon, Oxford, 1976. This forms the second volume of a revised and expanded version of the work on hydrothermal and magmatic deposits.

Annotated Bibliographies of Mineral Deposits in Europe, Part 1, Pergamon, Oxford, 1984.

Glossaries

Bates, R.L. and Jackson, J.A. *Glossary of Geology*, American Geological Institute, Falls Church, Va., 1980. As there is no large specifically mineralogical glossary, this very good geological one, with lots of mineral information, is a good substitute. It includes a large bibliography.

Lazarenko, E.K. and Vynar, O.M. *Mineralohichnyi Slovnyk*, Naukova Dumka, Kiev, 1985. The best guide for Russian and Ukrainian terms (often a headache); many are explained in English.

On-line Services

Those of most use to the mineralogist are the GeoRef and GeoArchive databases run by the DIALOG host in California. Users should contact a library with access to DIALOG. Within the database are up-to-date files of *Mineralogical Abstracts* (the DIALOG GeoBase file) and chemical abstracts, which contain a great deal of information on minerals. The GeoRef database is the on-line equivalent of *The Bibliography and Index of Geology*. In due course it may be possible to download data to personal discs. Some databases are now available on CD–ROM.

Journals for the Collector

Lapis published by Christian Weise Verlag, Munich, since 1976, deals mainly, but not exclusively, with German, Swiss and Austrian mineral deposits.

The Journal of the Russell Society is a quality
publication. It deals with British mineral
deposits, and papers are of a good scientific
standard. The society is loosely based at
Leicester University, England, and is the
country's only amateur mineralogical society
of standing.

Mineralogical Record, Tucson, Arizona, USA,
published since 1970 is the most generally
useful journal. It is a high-class production
aimed primarily at the well-educated
amateur and carries quality papers on a
variety of mineralogical topics (not lapidary).

Schweizer Strahler, published by Schweizerische
Vereinigung der Strahler und Mineralien-
sammler, Luzerne, Switzerland, since 1967, is
a more specialized journal dealing with
Alpine minerals. Papers in German or French
with translations in the other language.

More advanced journals

Many, if not most, of the papers in the following
journals are of a high scientific standard, and as
they deal with new discoveries and physical
properties with a certain amount of raw data, the
collector may find them rather daunting.
However, be consoled by the fact that no one
understands all the papers in any one issue. Have
a look next time you go to the library and, as
always, search the indexes to find references to
what you want.

American Mineralogist (Mineralogical Society of
America, Ann Arbor, Michigan) began in 1916
and is the official journal of the society. It is in
the front rank for publishing original
research.

The European Journal of Mineralogy, Société
Française de Minéralogie et de Cristallo-
graphie, Paris, 1984–, is a recently founded
publication, a combination of several
European mineralogical journals.

Mineralogical Magazine, Mineralogical Society,
London, has been published since 1876 and is
the 'senior' journal on the subject.

These and many other useful journals are abs-
tracted in *Mineralogical Abstracts*. These, with
many other sources of mineralogical and geological information, are also available on-line via
the DIALOG host. Major libraries, such as the
British Library and the Library of Congress, also
hold all the mineralogical and geological journals
likely to be needed, including the major ones from
non-English-speaking countries.

Abstracts

Those needing to consult papers in journals will
need to turn to abstracts to find out what has been
written. *Mineralogical Abstracts* has been published since 1920/22 by the Mineralogical Society,
London. *Referativnyi Zhurnal Geologiia*, founded
in 1956, covers Russian-language material, but
can be consulted only in very large libraries.
Although there are also French and German abstracts, it makes more sense to search on-line.

Maps

Blyth, F.G.H. *Geological Maps and their
Interpretation*, Arnold, London, 1965. A good
treatment of the interpretation of geological
maps.

British Library Catalogue of Maps, British Library,
London. A vital work for map listing.

Bibliographie Cartographique Internationale,
Librairie de la Faculté des Sciences, Paris,
1962–79.

See also the 'Kartografiya' section of *Referativnyi
Zhurnal Geografia* which is available separately.

Useful addresses

British Geological Survey, Nicker Hill,
Keyworth, Nottingham. There is an
information and sales point at Exhibition
Road, London for all BGS material.

British Library Science Reference and
Information Service, 9 Kean Street, London.
In general, books on mining are held at 25
Southampton Buildings, Chancery Lane,
London.

Mineralogical Society of Great Britain, 41
Queen's Gate, London.

Natural History Museum (British Museum of
Natural History), Cromwell Road, London.

Mineralogical Society of America, 1909 K Street
NW, Washington, DC.

Mineralogical Association of Canada, Royal
Ontario Museum, Dept of Mineralogy,
Toronto, Canada.

Mineralogical Society of Japan, Institute of
Mineralogy, Petrology and Economic Geology,
Tohoku University, Aobayama, Sendai, Japan.

GLOSSARY

Acicular Sharp, needle-like crystals

Adamantine Used of the highest degree of lustre possessed by the surface of a mineral. Normally used only for diamond

Amorphous Opposite of crystalline. Amorphous substances lack a regular internal atomic structure. Opal and glass are examples

Anion A negatively-charged ion

Anisotropic Crystals within which light travels at different velocities in different directions

Asterism A star-like effect seen usually by reflected light on the top of cabochon-cut gemstones and caused by oriented crystals of another mineral

Birefringence See Double refraction

Cabochon A gemstone cut without facets in a rounded and domed shape with a flat base

Cation A positively-charged ion

Chatoyancy Seen in some cabochon-cut gemstones in which a bright line of light traverses the long direction and is seen against a dark background

Cleavage A direction of atomic weakness seen only in crystals and along which a crystal may easily break

Complex ion Sometimes known as radicals, complex ions consist of sub-groups of atoms bonded strongly together, as in many silicates

Country rock The existing geological formation of an area

Covalent bonding Where two or more atoms share their electrons

Density The mass per unit volume of a substance

Double refraction In crystals other than those of the cubic system a ray of incident light is split in two on entering, each ray travelling through the crystal at a different velocity

Ductile Able to be drawn into a wire

Efflorescence A fluffy deposit of minute crystals formed by some minerals on rocks and mine equipment

Enantiomorphous Crystals with left- or right-handed forms, each the mirror image of the other. Quartz is the best example

Euhedral Crystals showing well-developed faces

Fluorescence The emission of radiation (usually visible light) when a substance is irradiated by higher-energy radiation such as ultra-violet light

Fracture Breakage not along a crystallographic direction

Fumarole A vent from which gases are emitted and characteristic of volcanic activity

Gangue Used to describe a mineral other than the one sought in a mining operation, especially those in which metallic ores are worked

Geode A cavity in a rock within which crystals grow towards the centre

Hand specimen A mineral large enough to be seen without magnification

Hydrothermal processes Formation of minerals from hot, mineralized watery solutions

Hopper crystal Hollowed-out crystals formed when edges grow in preference to faces

Interfacial angle The angle between adjacent faces on a crystal, measured from the angle between perpendiculars dropped to both faces

Inclusions Solid, liquid or gaseous material found inside a mineral

Ion An atom with an electrical charge

Ionic bonding Where two atoms bond together by transferring electrons from one to the other

Isomorphous Having the same crystal structure as another mineral, but a different chemical composition

Isomorphous series Two or more minerals may show physical and chemical variation along a smooth curve

Isotropic Crystals in which light travels at the same velocity, regardless of direction. Amorphous substances and crystals of the cubic system are isotropic

Lamellae Thin, leaf- or page-like mineral layers caused by repeated twinning

Lattice The three-dimensional and regularly repeating atomic arrangement of a crystal, each point in it having identical surroundings

Lustre The nature of a mineral surface from which light is reflected

Magma Molten rock beneath the crust of the earth

Malleable Able to be hammered out flat

Matrix The rock or other mineral in which a specimen is embedded

Metamorphism The alteration of existing rocks and their minerals by later geological activity

Native Used of metals to denote the uncombined element

Ore A metal found in large enough quantities to mine economically

Outcrop Rock appearing on the surface

Paragenesis The order in which a mineral crystallizes compared with its neighbours

Parting A direction of breakage in a crystal not along a direction of atomic weakness as in cleavage

Phosphorescence The continuation of fluorescence after the activating radiation is turned off

Pleochroism Showing different colours in different directions

Polarized light Light which vibrates in one direction only, parallel to the direction of travel

Polymorph A substance displaying several distinct forms, each having the same chemical composition

Pseudomorph A mineral taking on the shape of a previously existing mineral or organic substance is said to be pseudomorphous after that substance, e.g. opalized wood or shell

Precipitation The deposition of minerals from solution

Refraction The deviation of a ray of light from its path on entering a different transparent medium

Refractive index The ratio between the velocity of a ray of light in vacuo and its velocity within another medium

Space group One of 230 different ways in which atoms can be arranged in a homogeneous way in an actual or possible crystal structure

Specific gravity The ratio of the density of a mineral to the density of an equal volume of pure water

Streak The colour shown by the powder of a mineral when it is drawn over unglazed porcelain

Unit cell The basic unit of pattern in a crystal; the smallest grouping of atoms which, when repeated in all directions, makes up the complete crystal

Valency The number of electrons an atom must gain or lose to attain the configuration of the most similar inert gas

Vein Said of a mineral deposit cutting other rocks and arising from solutions

Vesicles Cavities in an igneous rock originating from bubbles within the lava from which the rock is formed

Zeolites A large family of hydrous alumino-silicates with an easy and reversible loss of their water of hydration

ACKNOWLEDGEMENTS

The author wishes to thank Dr Wendell E. Wilson and Dr Joel Arem for loaning the majority of the photographs illustrating this book. Thanks also extended to Mr Martin Pulsford, Natural History Museum, London.

Photographs appearing in this book are strictly copyright as follows:

© 1991 WENDELL E. WILSON
PAGES 5, 24/25, 35, 37, 53, 73, 74, 75, 76, 77, 78, 79, 80, 81, 83, 84, 85, 86, 87, 88, 90, 91, 93, 95, 96, 98, 99, 100, 102, 103, 105, 108, 109, 111, 113, 114, 117, 118, 119, 120, 122, 123, 125, 128, 130, 132, 134, 135, 136, 137, 138, 140, 143, 144, 145, 148, 149, 150, 152, 153, 154, 155, 157, 158, 159, 160, 161, 164, 165, 167, 168, 170/171

© 1991 JOEL AREM
PAGES 2, 6/7, 10/11, 12, 13, 14, 15, 16, 17, 18, 19 (ABOVE), 20, 21, 22, 23, 26/27, 28/29, 30, 32/33, 36, 38, 40/41, 42, 43, 44, 45, 48, 49, 50, 51, 52, 54, 55, 56/57, 58, 59, 60, 61, 62, 63, 64/65, 66, 67, 68, 69, 70/71, 82, 89, 92, 94, 97, 101, 106, 107, 110, 112, 115, 116, 121, 124, 126, 127, 129, 131, 133, 139, 141, 142, 146, 147, 151, 156, 162, 163, 166, 172/173, 174, 175, 176, 177, 178, 179, 180

BY COURTESY OF THE NATURAL HISTORY MUSEUM, LONDON
PAGES 8/9, 19 (BELOW)

© 1991 JOEL AREM
ENDPAPERS Lava flows, Yellowstone Park, USA

SPECIMENS FROM FOLLOWING COLLECTIONS
R. SULLIVAN: 5, 53; SMITHSONIAN INSTITUTION: 24–25, 37, 79, 87, 88, 95, 100, 103, 105 (BELOW), 108, 118, 120, 122, 130, 132, 143, 149, 150, 153, 170/171; W. Larson: 35, 81, 137, 167; A. E. SEAMAN MINERALOGICAL MUSEUM, MICHIGAN TECHNOLOGICAL UNIVERSITY, HOUGHTON: 73; HARVARD MINERALOGICAL MUSEUM: 74, 86 (BELOW), 93, 102, 105 (ABOVE), 138, 157; T. GRESSMAN: 75, 113; A. GRESSMAN: 161; F. J. BARLOW: 76; E. SCHLEPP: 78, 90, 98, 119, 128, 154; DENVER MUSEUM OF NATURAL HISTORY: 79, 119; L. PRESMYK: 80; F. CURETON: 83, 85, 86 (ABOVE), 109, 164; K. ROBERTS: 84, 99; B. DEWITT: 91; R. KOSNAR: 96; W. E. WILSON: 111, 123, 140, 165; J. ZWEIBEL: 114, 136, 158; NEW MEXICO SCHOOL OF MINES MINERAL MUSEUM, SOCORRO: 125; LOUISVILLE PUBLIC LIBRARY: 134 (ABOVE); REX HARRIS: 134 (BELOW); C. GRAEBER: 135 (LEFT); VAN SCRIVER: 135 (RIGHT); TIM SHERBURN: 144, 148, 168; R. TYSON: 145; E. BANCROFT: 152; C. BARBOSA: 155; W. SORENSON: 159; D. SHANNON: 160

PAGE 2 Rhodochrosite (South Africa)
PAGES 6/7 Entrenched meanders shown by a river in Utah, USA
PAGES 8/9 Slate (Wales)
PAGES 24/25 Turquoise (Virginia, USA)
PAGES 170/171 Torbernite (North Carolina, USA)

PAGES 46/47 Drawings by DAVID HENDERSON
PAGES 173–180 Information on deposits adapted from Peter Bancroft, *Gem and Crystal Treasures*, Western Enterprises, Fallbrook, California, and *Mineralogical Record*, 1984.

INDEX